SATs Like a NINJA

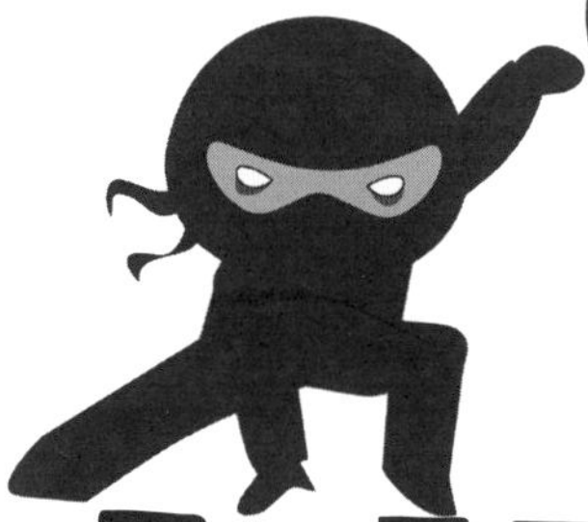

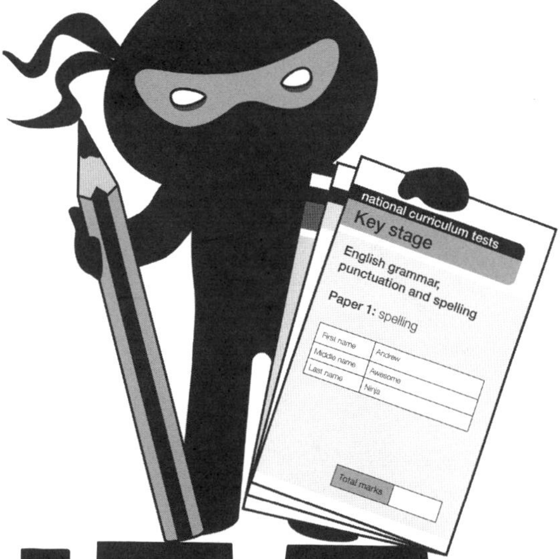

BLOOMSBURY EDUCATION
LONDON OXFORD NEW YORK NEW DELHI SYDNEY

BLOOMSBURY EDUCATION

Bloomsbury Publishing Plc
50 Bedford Square, London, WC1B 3DP, UK
29 Earlsfort Terrace, Dublin 2, Ireland

BLOOMSBURY, BLOOMSBURY EDUCATION and the Diana logo are trademarks of Bloomsbury Publishing Plc

First published in Great Britain, 2024 by Bloomsbury Publishing Plc

This edition published in Great Britain, 2024 by Bloomsbury Publishing Plc

Text copyright © Andrew Jennings, 2024

Andrew Jennings has asserted his right under the Copyright, Designs and Patents Act, 1988, to be identified as Author of this work

Material from Department for Education documents used in this publication are approved under an Open Government Licence: www.nationalarchives.gov.uk/doc/open-government-licence/version/3

Bloomsbury Publishing Plc does not have any control over, or responsibility for, any third-party websites referred to or in this book. All internet addresses given in this book were correct at the time of going to press. The author and publisher regret any inconvenience caused if addresses have changed or sites have ceased to exist, but can accept no responsibility for any such changes

All rights reserved. No part of this publication may be reproduced or transmitted in any form or by any means, electronic or mechanical, including photocopying, recording, or any information storage or retrieval system, without prior permission in writing from the publishers

A catalogue record for this book is available from the British Library

ISBN: PB: 978-1-8019-9201-5; ePDF: 978-1-8019-9202-2; ePub: 978-1-8019-9200-8

2 4 6 8 10 9 7 5 3 1

Text design by Jeni Child

Printed and bound in the UK by CPI Group Ltd, Croydon CR0 4YY

To find out more about our authors and books visit www.bloomsbury.com and sign up for our newsletters

Contents

What are **SATs**? 5
Timeline of the tests 6

SPAG 8
English grammar, punctuation
and spelling: Paper 1 10

GRAMMAR 12
Nouns 12
Adjectives 13
Verbs 14
Adverbs 15
Modal verbs 16
Co-ordinating conjunctions 17
Subordinating conjunctions 18
Pronouns 19
Relative pronouns, possessive pronouns
and relative clauses 20
Contractions 22
Articles and determiners 23
Prepositions and prepositional phrases 24
Adverbials, adverbial phrases and
fronted adverbials 25
Prefixes and suffixes 27
Noun phrases and expanded
noun phrases 29
Past, present and progressive
verb forms 30
Subject and object 32

Sentence types 33
Active and passive sentences 35
Formal and informal language /
Standard and non-Standard English 36
Synonyms and antonyms 37
Word classes 38
Subordinate and main clauses 40

PUNCTUATION 41
Capital letters and full stops 41
Commas 42
Apostrophes for possession
or contraction 43
Speech punctuation / inverted commas 45
Colon / semi-colon 46
Parenthesis 47

SPELLING 48
English grammar, punctuation
and spelling: Paper 2 48
Tricky spelling rules to remember 50

READING 52
English reading 52
Pre-reading a text and finding
key words 54
Skimming and scanning 57
Skimming and scanning: Images 58
Skimming and scanning: Timetables 59
Skimming and scanning: Text 60

Contents continued...

Key words in the question strategy 61
Retrieval 63
True or false questions 64
Find and copy questions 65
Multiple choice questions 66
Sequencing 68
Inference: Images 72
Inference: Thoughts 74
Inference: Explain 75
Inference: What does it suggest? 76
Two- and three- mark questions:
Using evidence to support 77
'What Impression' questions 79

MATHS 84
Mathematics: Paper 1 arithmetic 84
Addition 86
Subtraction 88
Place value missing number 90
Short division 91
Short multiplication 93
Decimal addition 94
Decimal subtraction from
whole numbers 95
Multiplying and dividing by 10, 100
and 1,000 96
Finding 10% and 5% (and multiples of 10)...... 98
Finding 1%, 2%, 3% and 4% 99
Finding complex percentages 100
Multiplying and dividing by 0 and 1 101
Square and cube numbers 102
Multiplying fractions 103
Dividing fractions by whole numbers 104
Multiplying fractions by whole numbers 105
Finding fractions of amounts 106

Adding and subtracting fractions
with the same denominator 108
Adding and subtracting fractions
with different denominators 109
Adding fractions and mixed numbers 111
Subtracting fractions from mixed
numbers 112
Adding and subtracting mixed numbers 113
Multiplying mixed numbers 115
BODMAS 116
Long multiplication 117
Long division 118

REASONING 120
Mathematics: Paper 2 and 3 reasoning 120
Number: Doubling and halving 122
Number: Multiples and related facts 123
Shape: 2D 124
Shape: 3D 125
Measure and volume 126
Time 128
Angles 130
Lines 131
Roman numerals 132
Money 133
Sequences 134
Perimeter and area 135
Multi-step problems 136

NOTES 140

What are SATs?

What?

Key Stage 2 SATs are the National Curriculum Assessments or Standard Assessment Tests that happen at the end of primary school for Year 6 pupils in England. The tests cover spelling, punctuation, grammar, reading and maths.

When?

Key Stage 2 SATs normally take place in early May after the school holidays. The tests start on the Monday of the testing week and run through until the Thursday. If pupils are unable to attend school due to illness or other issues, tests will be taken when they return to school. The tests are normally carried out first thing in the morning, but schools are free to choose when the test takes place.

Some schools choose to invite Year 6 children into school early each morning before the tests and provide breakfast for them. This is to allow pupils to arrive in good time, relax with their friends before the test and revise information that might be useful in the test that day.

Where?

The tests will normally be completed in school. Some schools administer the tests in a school hall, but more commonly schools will deliver the tests in multiple classrooms, libraries and other spaces in school. Schools often choose locations that children are familiar and comfortable with.

How?

SATs tests are paper booklets. Pupils are required to answer in the booklets using pencils, pens and other equipment that will be provided for them by the school, such as rulers and protractors. Pupils don't need to bring anything of their own to complete the tests.

Each test has a set time limit and will be completed under test conditions.

Members of staff who are leading the tests may read certain parts of questions to pupils, but not support or prompt a pupil's knowledge.

Why?

SATs are used to gauge whether pupils are leaving primary school and moving onto secondary school at an expected level or not. This is known as 'working at the expected standard'. Scores from the test tell you whether a pupil is working below, at or above this expected standard and whether they are ready to access learning at secondary school.

Scores

Marks from the test papers are converted into a score. Scores are given on a scale of 80 to 120, with a score of 100 or more meaning that a pupil is meeting the expected governmental standard (but this equates to different marks for each paper).

Timeline of the tests

Monday

Punctuation and grammar -
This paper has 50 questions.
Each question is worth one mark.

Spelling - This paper has 20 questions. Each question is worth one mark. This test is usually carried out straight after the Punctuation and Grammar paper.

Total marks for spelling, punctuation and grammar - 70 marks.

Tuesday

Reading - This paper has approximately 35 questions. Questions can be worth one, two or three marks.

Total marks for reading - 50 marks.

Wednesday

Maths - arithmetic (Paper 1) - This paper has 36 questions. Each question is worth one mark. This paper will contain two long multiplication and two long division questions, which are worth two marks each.

Maths - reasoning (Paper 2) - This paper has between 21 and 25 questions. Questions can be worth one, two or three marks.

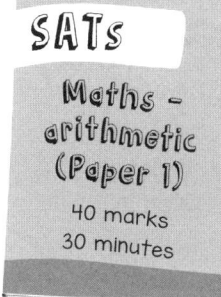

Thursday

Maths - reasoning (Paper 3) - This paper has between 21 and 25 questions. Questions can be worth one, two or three marks.

Total marks for maths - 110 marks.

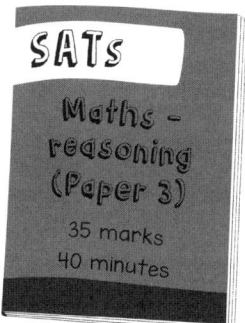

Friday

No tests today. Relax, you are finished!

Top 10 Ninja SATs preparation tips

1. Let's make a revision date

Time for a routine! Plan a little study time each day - short sessions work way better than last-minute craziness. Try to stick to 15-20 minutes max. But remember, your school will be doing everything to get you ready for SATs, so try not to worry about it!

2. Create your super study zone

Find a cosy spot with good light for your study adventures. Less distraction, more focus!

3. Get past papers in the game

Practice makes perfect, right? Try out some past papers to get the hang of how things work. It's like a sneak peek into the SATs world. Search for 'KS2 SATs Papers' online; there are many websites where you can download these for free.

4. Put your phone and tablets away!

Phones, tablets and tech can be a major distraction. So, if you're working in smart 15-20 blocks, just leave your gadgets in another room.

5. Books, books and more books

Dive into cool stories and interesting facts. Mix it up with different kinds of books. Reading makes your brain super strong!

6 See the whole picture

Remember, the SATs tests check your learning from Year 3 to Year 6, so lots of the content is quite simple. You already know most of it, so don't overcomplicate things. Use SATs Like a Ninja to focus on the areas you don't feel confident with.

7 Get moving with revision

Active learning is like a superhero move for your brain! Mix it up by creating some flashcards, or why not try teaching stuff to your buddy or even your pet?

8 Fuel your brain with good stuff

Eat well, sleep tight and keep active. Your brain loves it when you treat it right. Healthy choices equal super study powers! Drink water, get as much sleep as possible and get outside and exercise.

9 You're a learning superstar

Mistakes are just stepping stones to being a genius. Keep going, and remember, you're a learning ninja in the making!

10 Chill time is a must

Break time! Plan breaks during study sessions, and make sure you have time for your favourite stuff and most importantly, get outside. A happy mind is a smart mind!

You've got this! SATs are just a little adventure on your learning journey. Stay positive, do your best, and don't forget to high-five yourself for being awesome!

SPAG

English grammar, punctuation and spelling: Paper 1

Test details

Test day - Monday

Time allowed - 45 minutes

Number of questions - 50 questions. Each question is worth one mark. 50 marks total.

The marks for this paper are combined with the marks for the spelling paper to give a combined grammar, punctuation and spelling mark out of 70.

Layout and appearance

The grammar and punctuation paper looks like this. You will find multiple questions on each page.

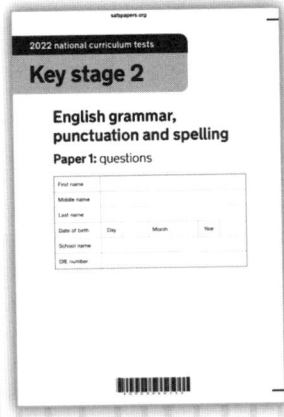

Example questions

The grammar and punctuation paper asks you to answer questions in different ways. It might ask you to tick a box, circle a word or phrase, underline a word or phrase, and so on.

49 Tick one box in each row to show which form of the verb is underlined in each sentence.

Sentence	Simple past	Past progressive	Past perfect
Nathan had hoped for a part in the school play.			
The children were rehearsing their lines.			
Lots of parents came to watch.			

1 mark

36 Which option makes the sentence start with an **adverbial**?

_____ we lined up for the class photo.

Tick **one**.

It was noisy and crowded, but ☐
The photographer arrived while ☐
With big smiles on our faces, ☐
The whole class were ready so ☐

1 mark

NINJA TIP:

It's really important to answer the question in the way in which you are asked to. If it asks you to circle a word, you need to circle a word.

33 Circle the **relative pronoun** in the sentence below.

The children who were going swimming had their lunch earlier than we did.

1 mark

24 Underline the **subordinate clause** in the sentence below.

When the crowd heard the clattering sound, they gasped in astonishment.

1 mark

Grammar

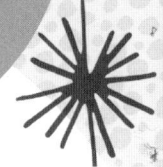

Nouns

Nouns are naming words. Nouns are used to name and identify people, places, objects and even feelings. There are three different types of nouns that you need to know:

Proper noun
Proper nouns are nouns that require capital letters because they are the name of a person (David, Lisa), a place (England, Rochdale) or an other official title (Nike, Apple, Samsung).

Common noun
Common nouns name everything we can see. Everything around you that you can see is a common noun. For example, table, chair, window, bottle, wall, T-shirt, teacher... everything! These are very obvious and very common.

Abstract noun
Abstract nouns are less obvious and name feelings or emotions. For example, love, pride, shock, talent. A good way to think about abstract nouns is that you can't touch them.

Examples

Andrew and Jessica walked to the park to walk the dog.

The children heard a rumour that Alex Walker was visiting the school.

Six birds sat next to the window, which gave Mia lots of pleasure.

NINJA TIP:
Articles and determiners (see p. 23) will often come before nouns, with articles being a, an, the.

 SATs example
Circle the four **nouns** in the sentence below.

The strength of the wind made the trees in the forest sway and bend.

strength, wind, trees, forest

SATS TIP
In the SATs, there may be questions where you need to find the nouns in a sentence. Remember, there could be more than one to find.

SATs example
Circle the three **nouns** in the sentence below.

The fire gave the room a cosy feeling.

fire, room, feeling

Adjectives

Adjectives are used to describe nouns (see p. 12) and pronouns (see p. 19). Adjectives are very common and help to add more information about a noun or pronoun. Visualise the following:

red ball   scary monster   large vehicle

> **NINJA TIP:**
> Adjectives are sometimes tricky to spot. As adjectives describe nouns and pronouns, an easy way to spot an adjective is to find the noun first, then look for words that describe that noun.

Examples

In these examples, the nouns are highlighted. The adjectives describing the nouns are underlined.

Thea was wearing a red dress and her hair was curly.

A strong wind blew the wooden door wide open.

The screaming children ran onto the playground, which was slippery.

 SATs questions might ask you to find many adjectives in a sentence.

Circle the three **adjectives** in the sentence below.

He made his way up the cobbled street, striding like the bold and determined man he was.

---

cobbled, bold, determined

Practice TASK

1 Write a list of ten nouns. Add an adjective to each noun that describes it.

2 Use these adjective and noun combinations in a sentence.

Verbs

Verbs are words that describe an action — a physical action, mental action or just a state of existing. Verbs are required for a sentence to be formed.

Examples

In these examples, the nouns are highlighted. The verbs are in bold.

Harry **ran** into the classroom and **dumped** his coat on the floor.

The sun **rose** above the mountains and **warmed** the ground below.

The wolf **stalked** its prey across the meadow, until it finally **pounced**.

Auxiliary verbs

Although you're unlikely to be tested on these, auxiliary verbs or 'helping verbs' such as were, is, was, are, have, can and has, are still classed as verbs. See 'were' in the SATs example below.

SATs TIP
Spotting nouns can make it easier to spot verbs, as the verb usually describes an action that the noun or pronoun (subject) is performing.

NINJA TIP:
Verbs can vary depending on how they are used in a sentence. For example, **jump**, **jumps**, **jumped** and **jumping** are all verbs.

Practice TASK

1. Read a few pages of a book. As you read, spot the verbs. Each sentence should contain at least one. Books are great for endless verb spotting!

2. Write three sentences. Once finished, circle the verbs and highlight the nouns.

SATs example
Circle the four **verbs** in the passage below.

There were hundreds of gulls circling in the sky.

They gathered near the dock, searching for scraps.

were, circling, gathered, searching

Adverbs

Adverbs most commonly describe verbs and tell us more about how the verb (action) is being performed. Adverbs can also describe adjectives and other adverbs.

SATS TIP
Adverbs often end in -ly, but not always! If you are not sure how to spot them, check out the Ninja Tip. Remember: adverbs add to the verb.

Examples

Try to spot the verb first and then spotting the adverb will be much easier. In these examples, the verbs are in bold. The adverbs have a dotted line underneath.

The team **darted** quickly out onto the muddy sports pitch.

Esther aimlessly **wandered** through the woods.

Julian **ran** hard into the gale force wind and rain.

NINJA TIP:
If you are unsure about identifying an adverb, try to spot the verb first. If you can pick out the verb, you can then look for a word close by that gives more information about the verb (action).

SATs example
Tick the **adverb** in the sentence below.

Tick **one**.

The lively crowd cheered loudly when the rally car race began.

loudly

SATs example
Circle the three **adverbs** in the sentence below.

Because it was raining hard, the driver was unable to see clearly and almost crashed his shiny car.

hard, clearly, almost

Practice TASK

1. Use the internet to search for common adverbs. Create a poster about all of the common adverbs you have found. Include two or three example sentences in your poster showing adverbs in action.

Modal verbs

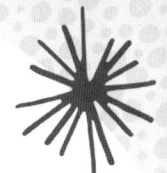

Modal verbs suggest possibility and give the reader an understanding of how likely something is to happen. The great thing about modal verbs is there aren't too many and they are easy to remember. Here's a few of the main ones.

can could must shall should would
may might ought to will need

NINJA TIP:
Some modal verbs, like **will** and **can't**, show a high level of certainty, whereas words like **might**, **could** and **should** are uncertain and could go either way.

Examples

The modal verbs in these examples have been highlighted.

I think Ruby is worried because we may get caught.

Hamed said that he might come out to play later.

Do you think we should go in?

SATs example

Circle the **modal verb** in the sentence below.

Kate hoped that she would see goats and sheep at the farm.

would

SATS TIP

Some modal verb questions might ask you to explain how different modal verbs change the meaning of a sentence.

1) Yusuf and his sister go swimming with their dad.

2) Yusuf and his sister might go swimming with their dad.

In the second sentence, the use of **might** suggests that it is not certain that they will go swimming. In the first sentence, it is certain that they go swimming.

16

Co-ordinating conjunctions

Co-ordinating conjunctions are much simpler than they sound. Co-ordinating conjunctions join two words, two phrases or two clauses together.

Joining words

The sun was bright and warm.

My ice-cream was cold yet delicious.

I would like pizza or pasta for lunch.

Joining phrases

He was excited for the concert but nervous about the noise.

We can walk to the park or drive to the pool.

Joining clauses

A simple explanation of a clause is a group of words that contain a subject and verb, and could form a simple sentence. A co-ordinating conjunction joins two of these clauses together.

The **rain hammered** down on the roof, and the **wind battered** the windows with debris.

                      clause 1   cc   clause 2

NINJA TIP: There are only seven co-ordinating conjunctions to focus on for SATs and it's easy to remember all seven using the mnemonic FANBOYS:

F - for, **A** - and, **N** - nor, **B** - but, **O** - or, **Y** - yet, **S** - so

SATs example Most SATs question ask you to circle the co-ordinating conjunction or add the correct one to a sentence.

> Circle the **co-ordinating conjunction** in the sentence below.
>
> If you want to enter the competition, you can send your idea by email or by post.

or

> Circle the **co-ordinating conjunction** in the sentence below.
>
> I started drawing a car, but then I changed my mind because I had a better idea.

but

Subordinating conjunctions

Subordinating conjunctions start subordinate clauses and help to form part of a complex sentence. A subordinate clause links to a main clause and relies on the main clause to make sense. Subordinate clauses cannot stand alone as a sentence.

I wanted to visit the beach, although I don't really enjoy being hot.
    main clause   sc   subordinate clause

SUBORDINATING CONJUNCTION WORD BANK

after	how	unless
although	if	until
as	since	when
because	than	where
before	though	while

SATS TIP
Watch out for subordinate clauses starting sentences, when the subordinate clause comes before the main clause.

Examples

He came to school, although he felt sick.

If you win the tournament, I will buy you a treat after school.

Since it will be very hot today, we will visit the beach.

SATs example
Insert a **subordinating conjunction** to show that we ate lunch and listened to music at the same time.

We listened to the music _____ we ate our lunch.

while, as

SATs example
Complete the sentence below with an appropriate **subordinating conjunction**.

_____ we ate our lunch.

although, since

SATs example
Circle the **subordinating conjunction** in the sentence below.

Since it is sunny today, we can play rounders or cricket.

since

Pronouns

Pronouns replace nouns. Pronouns help to avoid repetition. For example, rather than using the noun Amelia repetitively in a sentence, we can use a pronoun to replace it:

Amelia loves going for walks, and she loves swimming in the sea.

Rather than repeating 'Amelia', we can use 'she' instead.

PRONOUN WORD BANK	I me	you your	they their	them his	him her	she it	us we

Examples

The gang decided to adventure through the swamp, until they became lost.

Since Jessica was no longer able to attend the party, she decided to clean her room.

SATS TIP
Pronoun questions in SATs often ask you to replace nouns with the correct pronoun.

SATs example

Replace the underlined words with the correct **pronoun**. Write one pronoun in each box.

When Jack's grandmother came to stay, she gave Jack some money.

Jack used his money to buy a game called Gables. Jack could not

wait to get home and play the new game.

him, he, it

Relative pronouns, possessive pronouns and relative clauses

Relative pronouns

Relative pronouns are pronouns that are used to mark the beginning of a relative clause. Relative clauses are a group of words that relate to and modify a noun.

RELATIVE PRONOUN WORD BANK
who, which, that, whom, whose

Examples

My neighbour, who is 83, has just flown to Dubai.

I met Samiha in town yesterday, which was a nice surprise.

SATs example

Circle the **relative pronoun** in the sentence below.

The children who were going swimming had their lunch earlier than we did.

who

SATs example

Insert a **relative pronoun** to complete the sentence below.

Everyone loved the music _____ was played last night.

that

SATs example

Circle the **relative pronoun** in the sentence below.

The mountain, which could be seen in the distance, had snow on top of it.

which

Possessive pronouns

Possessive pronouns are pronouns that refer to possession or ownership.

Examples

The red book in the pile is <u>mine</u>.

Shall we go to <u>your</u> house after school?

POSSESSIVE PRONOUN WORD BANK

mine, yours, his, hers, ours, yours, theirs

Circle the **possessive pronoun** in the sentence below.

The house next to ours, which belongs to Mrs Green, is for sale.

ours

Relative clauses

A relative clause uses a relative pronoun (who, which, that) to create a clause that adds further detail about a noun. Without the relative clause, the remainder of the sentence will normally still make sense.

Complete the sentence below with a **relative clause**. Remember to punctuate your answer correctly.

His sister, _____, is learning to speak Polish.

who is called Anna

Underline the **relative clause** in the sentence below.

The old house that is next to our school is for sale.

that is next to our school

Contractions

The word contraction means 'to shorten'. So, contractions in English are just two words that have been joined together and shortened. We use an apostrophe to show the letter or letters that have been removed.

do not	don't	would not	wouldn't
will not	won't	could not	couldn't
cannot	can't	should not	shouldn't
did not	didn't	must not	mustn't
is not	isn't	would have	would've
shall not	shan't	could have	could've
have not	haven't	should have	should've
they are	they're	must have	must've

NINJA TIP:
In the SATs paper, contractions will likely be referred to as the 'contracted form'.

SATS TIP
Sometimes SATs papers may show contracted forms of words and ask you to change them back to 'expanded form'. Don't worry, expanded form is just the two original words. So, 'don't' would go back to 'do not'. 'You've' would expand to 'you have'.

Examples

Mina knew that they hadn't (had not) packed enough supplies for the trip.

Everyone knew that Emily couldn't (could not) keep a secret.

SATs example

Write the **contracted form** of the underlined words in the box below.

We shall not do that again!
↓
[ ]

shan't

SATs example

Replace the underlined words in the sentences below with their **expanded forms**.

We're going into town later, so I'll buy some bread then.
↓ ↓
[ ] [ ]

We won't be back late.
↓
[ ]

We are, I will, will not

Articles and determiners

Determiners are words that come before a noun to quantify it or to show what the noun is referring to. Articles are a form of determiner.

Articles

are easy because there are only three to remember: **a, an, the**

Determiners

There are three other types of determiners:

Demonstratives - **this, that, these, those**

Possessives - **my, your, his, her, its, our, their**

Quantifiers - **common examples include many, much, more, most, some**

SATS TIP
Remember, articles and determiners will come before a noun to help clarify the noun in its context.

Examples

Our → dog and the → cat of my → neighbour were hiding in a → bush.
An → elephant wandered between the → trees and ate six → bananas.
Your → friend took my → orange and exchanged it for an → apple.

SATs example

Circle the three **determiners** in the sentence below.

William didn't have any cereal in the house, so he went out to buy some cornflakes.

any, the, some

SATs example

Circle the two **determiners** in the sentence below.

In an hour, we will be getting on our train.

an, our

Practice TASK

1 Read a few pages of a book. As you read each page, look for the nouns and the different determiners/articles that come before.

Prepositions and prepositional phrases

Prepositions

Prepositions are words that show position, movement, direction, time, place and location.

NINJA TIP:
Look at the word 'pre**position**': the word 'position' is a big clue to help remind you of what prepositions show us.

PREPOSITION WORD BANK

above	before	down	on
across	behind	from	to
against	below	in	toward
along	beneath	into	under
among	beside	near	upon
around	between	of	with
at	by	off	within

Examples

The boys ran <u>over</u> the bridge, jumped <u>onto</u> the wall and then hid <u>behind</u> the trees.

Christina stepped <u>down</u> <u>from</u> the stage and walked <u>across</u> the hall <u>towards</u> her teacher.

SATs example

Circle the four **prepositions** in the sentence below.

On a mountain bike, you can cycle across rocky ground, along muddy paths and over harsh terrain.

on, across, along, over

SATS TIP
SATs questions often want you to find multiple prepositions in one sentence. You need to find all of them to get one mark. See the SATs example to the left.

Prepositional phrases

A prepositional phrase is group of words that is made up of a preposition and the object of the preposition.

NINJA TIP:
A preposition will normally be the first word in a prepositional phrase.

Examples

The boys ran <u>over the bridge</u>, jumped <u>onto the wall</u> and then hid <u>behind the trees</u>.

Christina stepped <u>down from the stage</u> and walked <u>across the hall</u>.

Adverbials, adverbial phrases and fronted adverbials

Adverbials and adverbial phrases

Adverbials are used to explain how, where or when something happened.

Examples

In these examples, the adverbial phrases are underlined by a dotted line and the verbs being described are in bold.

Alice needed to **get** a drink in the middle of the night.
(The adverbial phrase modifies/describes when they got a drink.)

They **sailed** their boat with concentration and skill.
(The adverbial phrase modifies/describes how they sailed.)

They settled down and **built** a fire close to the ocean.
(The adverbial phrase modifies/describes where they built the fire.)

SATs example

Underline the **adverbial** in the sentence below.

On Wednesday, Felix has a dental appointment.

On Wednesday

SATs example

Underline the **adverbial** in the sentence below.

Last week, Ruby went swimming and played football.

Last week

SATs example

Which option makes the sentence start with an **adverbial**?

_____ we lined up for the class photo.

Tick **one**.

- It was noisy and crowded, but ☐
- The photographer arrived while ☐
- With big smiles on our faces, ☐
- The whole class were ready so ☐

With big smiles on our faces,

Fronted adverbials

Fronted adverbials are just adverbials that have been moved to the start of a sentence. They must be marked with a comma at the end of them.

Examples

In these examples, the adverbial phrases are underlined by a dotted line and the verbs being described are in bold.

In the middle of the night, Alice needed to **get** a drink. (When)
With concentration and skill, they **sailed** their boat. (How)
Close to the ocean, they settled down and **built** a fire. (Where)

SATS TIP
If you suspect that there is an adverbial phrase in the middle of a sentence, try moving the adverbial to the start. If the sentence still makes sense, you are probably right.

NINJA TIP: SATs questions might ask you to identify an adverbial in a sentence. Remember, this could still be a fronted adverbial.

SATs example

Insert a **comma** after the **fronted adverbial** in each sentence.

Luckily for us the ball rolled slowly past the goal.

After three hours of hard work the builders managed to dig out the tree.

1 mark

Prefixes and suffixes

Prefixes are added to the beginning of a word to change the meaning of the original or root word.

Suffixes are added to the end of a root word and also change the meaning and the word class. To the right is a small selection of common prefixes and suffixes.

PREFIX WORD BANK

aero-	de-	inter-	sub-
anti-	dis-	mis-	ultra-
auto-	en-	pre-	un-
co-	il-	re-	up-

SUFFIX WORD BANK

-able	-ian	-ive
-ed	-ible	-ship
-ful	-ing	-sion
-hood	-ist	-tion

Examples

Prefixes have specific meanings. For example, **re-** means 'again', so when we add **re-** to a word, we can understand the new meaning.

play → replay - means to play <u>again</u>

record → rerecord - means to record <u>again</u>

arrange → rearrange - means to arrange <u>again</u>

The prefix **dis-** means 'opposite of', 'not', 'remove' or 'reverse'.

agree → disagree - means do <u>not</u> agree

obey → disobey - means do <u>not</u> obey

honest → dishonest - means is <u>not</u> honest

SATs example

Draw a line to match each **prefix** to the correct word to make a new word.

Prefix	Word
en	cover
de	large
dis	frost

en-large, de-frost, dis-cover

SATs example

Draw a line to match each word to its correct **suffix**.

Words	Suffix
child	
champion	hood
neighbour	
friend	ship
member	

childhood, championship, neighbourhood, friendship, membership

SATs example

Draw a line to match each word to a **suffix** to make four different words. Use each suffix only once.

Word	Suffix
social	ish
relation	al
child	ise
season	ship

28

Noun phrases and expanded noun phrases

A noun phrase is a small group of words that contain a noun, but do not contain a verb.

Examples

I played on <u>the beach</u>.

Tilly ran to <u>the shop</u>.

<u>My dog</u> was very tired.

SATS TIP
Spot the nouns first, then look for any other words around the noun that add more information about it. Commonly, when we have more than two adjectives in an expanded noun phrase, a comma is used to separate them.

Expanded noun phrases are where the noun phrase has been expanded by the use of one or more adjectives, nouns or prepositions.

Examples

I played on <u>the warm, sandy beach with my friends</u>.

Tilly ran to <u>the sweet shop at the end of our road</u>.

<u>My old, lazy dog</u> was very tired.

NINJA TIP:
A noun phrase is group of words acting as a single noun.

SATs example

What is the grammatical term for the underlined words in the sentence below?

<u>The new paintbrushes</u> are in the box.

An expanded noun phrase

Past, present and progressive verb forms

Verbs can appear in many different forms, depending on the tense they are used in. It is important to be accurate with our tense and our verb form choices.

Simple present - Sam **plays** rugby.

Simple past - Sam **played** rugby.

Present progressive - Sam **is playing** rugby.

Past progressive - Sam **was playing** rugby.

Past perfect - Sam **has played** rugby.

NINJA TIP:
When reading a sentence, first try to think about whether it is written in the past or present tense.

SATS TIP
'Progressive form' sounds complicated, but it just refers to a verb that is in the process of happening or yet to finish:

Sam **was playing** rugby, when a dog ran on the pitch.

Although it is in the past, the event is ongoing when the dog interrupts the game, and so this verb form is past progressive.

SATs example

Complete the sentences below, using the **simple past tense** of the verbs in the boxes.

It was a cold day when we _____ handball.

[play]

My friend _____ the ball to me and I _____ it.

[throw]   [catch]

played, threw, caught

30

SATs example

Tick one box in each row to show whether the sentence is in the **present progressive** or the **past progressive**.

Sentence	Present progressive	Past progressive
Joey was playing football in the park after school.		
Joey's football skills are improving all the time.		
Joey is hoping to be a professional footballer.		

past progressive, present progressive, present progressive

SATs example

Tick one box in each row to show which form of the verb is underlined in each sentence.

Sentence	Simple past	Past progressive	Past perfect
Nathan <u>had hoped</u> for a part in the school play.			
The children <u>were rehearsing</u> their lines.			
Lots of parents <u>came</u> to watch.			

past perfect, past progressive, simple past

Subject and object

The subject and the object are both nouns in a sentence. The subject is the main noun and is the noun that is performing (the doer) the verb in the sentence, whereas the object is involved but not carrying out the action.

> **SATS TIP**
> The subject and object will always be nouns. Remember, the subject is the one who is the doer and will perform the verb/action. Spotting the main verb will help too.

Examples

Terry **made** scones.
In this example the verb is **made**. Who made the scones? Terry. So, Terry is the subject. The scones are the object.

All of a sudden, the wind **blasted** the trees and knocked them down.
In this example, the verb is **blasted**. Who or what blasted the trees? The wind. So, the wind is the subject. The trees are the object.

Violet was **pushed** by Alexander.
In this example, the verb is **pushed**. Who is doing the pushing? Alexander. So, Alexander is the subject. Violet is the object; she is being pushed.

SATS example

Label each box with **subject (S)** or **object (O)**.

Sam baked cakes for charity and he sold them at breaktime.

subjects are Sam and he, objects are cakes and them

> **NINJA TIP:**
> The subject doesn't always come first. The tense in which the sentence is written can affect this. Remember, focus on the verb, and who/what is 'doing' it.

SATS example

Underline the **subject** of the sentence below.

A whale lives in the sea.

A whale

32

Sentence types

There are four types of sentences that we need to know: statement, question, exclamation and command.

Statement

Statements give us information or tell us what might be happening.

The sun is shining in the sky.

Michael is wearing a red jumper.

Question

As expected, questions ask a question, as they require an answer, and end with a question mark: ?

What time is lunch?   Can I ride my bicycle?

Exclamation

Exclamations show strong feelings like happiness, shock or excitement.

What an amazing day!   How rude!

Command

A command tells you or someone else what to do. They can sometimes end in an exclamation mark.

Sit down on your chair now.   Finish your dinner and clean the table.

SATS TIP
Exclamation sentences often begin with 'what' or 'how'.

NINJA TIP:
Commands will usually start with an imperative verb (a 'bossy verb') — this can be a great clue to help you spot a command.

SATs example

> Tick **one** box in each row to show whether the sentence is a **question**, a **statement** or a **command**.

Sentence	Question	Statement	Command
In autumn, many trees lose their leaves			
Look at the trees carefully			
Scientists are studying how trees can live for thousands of years			
How can you tell a tree's age			

statement, command, statement, question

SATs example

> Draw a line to match each sentence to its correct **function**.
> Use each function box only **once**.

Sentence		Function
I expect the weather to be fine at the weekend		question
Are we likely to have good weather this weekend		command
Check the weather before deciding where to go		statement
What fantastic weather we have had this year		exclamation

statement, question, command, exclamation

Active and passive sentences

A sentence is written in the active voice when the subject of the sentence is performing the action. A sentence is written in the passive voice when the subject of the sentence has something done to it by someone or something.

Examples

Active: The dog chased the cat.

Passive: The cat was chased by the dog.

Active: Jason kicked the ball.

Passive: The ball was kicked by Jason.

SATS TIP
SATs questions often ask you to rewrite a sentence from active to passive, or from passive to active.

SATs example

Rewrite the sentence below so that it is in the **active voice**.
Remember to punctuate your sentence correctly.

The results were announced by the judges.

_____

The judges announced the results.

SATs example

Tick **one** box in each row to show whether the sentence is written in the **active voice** or the **passive voice**.

Sentence	Active	Passive
Otters live in clean rivers.		
Fish are eaten by otters.		
Usually, otters are playful creatures.		

active, passive, active

35

Formal and informal language/ Standard and non-Standard English

Standard or formal English is a form of English that is known around the world and that follows the correct grammatical rules. Non-Standard or informal English is more relaxed and might contain slang, abbreviations and other non-standard features.

> **SATS TIP**
> Contractions are informal. If you see a contraction in a sentence, usually this would indicate that the sentence is informal. Exact vocabulary will also be present in Standard English.

Examples

Standard/formal

'Good morning, Jim. How are you? What are your plans for today?'

'The football game is postponed until tomorrow due to severe weather conditions.'

Non Standard/informal

'Hey Jim. You OK? What are you up to today?'

'The match is off until tomorrow due to rubbish weather.'

SATs example

Which sentence is the most **formal**?

Tick **one**.

Your presence is requested at the wedding of our daughter.	☐
We'd love you to join us for our daughter's wedding.	☐
Our daughter's getting married – please come!	☐

Your presence is requested...

SATs example

Tick one box in each row to show whether the sentence is written in **Standard** or **non-Standard English**.

Sentence	Standard English	Non-Standard English
We was helping to design the new school building.		
He doesn't know nothing about football.		
I have done all the washing up.		

Standard English, Non-Standard English, Standard English

Synonyms and antonyms

Synonyms are words that have the same or almost the same meaning as another word. Antonyms are words that have the opposite meaning of another word.

> **SATS TIP**
> Often, these questions will use vocabulary that you may be unfamiliar with. Look out for these unfamiliar words, as they might help you spot the right words.

Examples

Synonym - same or very close meaning

If they could just <u>find</u> the clue on the map, they might be able to <u>discover</u> the treasure.

Freddy was <u>exhausted</u> from the race; Jeremy was <u>spent</u> too.

Antonym - opposite or close opposite meaning

The king announced that all of the <u>captive</u> soldiers were now <u>free</u>.

Tom was <u>excited</u> to read the new book, although after a few pages he was <u>disappointed</u>.

SATs example

Circle the two words that are **synonyms** of each other in the passage below.

The school will supply all meals during the trip. If parents wish to provide children with additional drinks, they may do so.

supply, provide

SATs example

Circle the two words that are **antonyms** in the sentence below.

What looked like a worthless collection of rusty metal turned out to include ancient coins and valuable jewellery.

worthless, valuable

Word classes

In SATs, there are lots of questions that ask you to identify the word class of a word or multiple words in a sentence.

SATS TIP
Normally these questions use unfamiliar vocabulary. Don't let it put you off; think nouns, verbs and adjectives.

Practice TASK

Take sentences from a book and identify the following word classes:

- Nouns
- Adjectives (if any)
- Verbs
- Adverbs (if any)
- Articles/determiners
- Conjunctions
- Prepositions

Being able to spot these word classes will put you in a really great place to answer questions. Practice with lots of different sentences will help. Just copy out sentences from books you have at home or school.

Examples

Jeremy quickly jumped over the wall and ran towards the shimmering ocean.
  N   Adv   V   P   N   C   V   P   A   N

NINJA TIP:
Go back to basics. Read the sentence and circle the nouns in the sentence. If you can spot the nouns, you can then spot adjectives. Remember, adjectives describe nouns – even if the vocabulary is unfamiliar, you can still see that it is describing the noun and so it must be an adjective.

SATs example

What are the **word classes** of the two underlined words in the sentence below?

The <u>erosive</u> force of the sea <u>erodes</u> the coastline.

		Tick **one**.
noun	adjective	☐
adjective	verb	☐
noun	verb	☐
adjective	adverb	☐

adjective, verb

SATs example

What is the **word class** of the underlined words in the sentence below?

<u>The</u> girl brought <u>a</u> sandwich and <u>an</u> apple to eat for lunch.

Tick **one**.
- adjectives ☐
- adverbs ☐
- determiners ☐
- nouns ☐

determines

SATs example

What is the **word class** of the underlined word in the sentence below?

The alarm rang and Jamal <u>immediately</u> jumped out of bed.

Tick **one**.
- conjunction ☐
- adverb ☐
- verb ☐
- determiner ☐

adverb

Subordinate and main clauses

Main and subordinate clauses are the two parts that make up a complex sentence. A main clause could operate as a sentence on its own, whereas a subordinate clause needs the main clause to make sense.

> **SATS TIP**
> Identify the subordinate clause by looking for a subordinating conjunction (see p. 18). Subordinate clauses begin with a subordinating conjunction.

Examples

Internet shopping is very popular today **because** it is convenient.

Because he was burnt by the sun, he went to the hospital.

Although she prepared her speech many times, Mary failed the test.

While waiting for the school bus, Emile ate his breakfast.

SATs example

Underline the **subordinate clause** in the sentence below.

When the crowd heard the clattering sound, they gasped in astonishment.

When the crowd heard the clattering sound

SATs example

Label each of the clauses in the sentence below as either **main (M)** or **subordinate (S)**.

After they had been for a swim, the boys had a drink because they were very thirsty.

S, M, S

SATs example

Tick one box in each row to show whether the underlined clause is a **main clause** or a **subordinate clause**.

Sentence	Main clause	Subordinate clause
The school, <u>which has three playing fields</u>, opened in 1967.		
Although I had cycled to school, <u>I still had the energy for my lessons.</u>		
<u>We will be proud</u> if we try our best.		

subordinate clause, main clause, main clause

40

Punctuation

Capital letters and full stops

Capital letter and full stop questions are very common. Capital letters are used to mark the beginning of a sentence and a full stop marks the end of a sentence.

Examples

Today is Michael's football birthday party at Strike. Todd, Ismail and Cho are coming from Doncaster on the train.

Tuesday and Wednesday are my favourite days of the week because Mia and I go dancing after school. Sometimes we see Mrs Roberts there as she is a dance teacher at Capital Dance Studios.

NINJA TIP:
Look out for proper nouns (names of people, places, businesses) as they also need capital letters, e.g. Fred, Manchester, Ford.

SATS TIP
SATs questions will often ask you to punctuate a passage. This might be one or several sentences. Try to read the passage aloud. Listen out for the natural pauses where a full stop would normally be.

SATs example

Insert **full stops** and **capital letters** in the passage below so that it is punctuated correctly.

Frogs are amphibians they live on land but they lay their eggs in water their eggs are called frogspawn during the winter, frogs hibernate at the bottom of ponds or in compost heaps

> Frogs are amphibians. They live on land but they lay their eggs in water. Their eggs are called frogspawn. During the winter, frogs hibernate at the bottom of ponds or in compost heaps.

SATs example

Circle each word that should begin with a **capital letter** in the sentence below.

when we visited the museum in birmingham, gareth arranged to travel by train with aunt laura.

> When, Birmingham, Gareth, Aunt Laura

Commas

Commas can be used in many ways. The three most common ways that commas come up in SATs are:

- Commas can be used to mark fronted adverbials.
- Commas can be used in pairs to mark an embedded clause.
- Commas can be used to list items.

Fronted adverbials

As the sun slowly rose, the explorers extinguished the fire and moved on.

Embedded clauses

Micah was visiting his uncle, although he didn't want to, with his parents.

SATS TIP
If you delete or remove the embedded clause, the sentence should make sense without it.

Lists

Aliyah quickly threw her red trainers, old running socks, water bottle **and** headphones into her sports bag.

NINJA TIP:
With commas in a list, the final two items are separated with 'and' not a comma.

Fronted adverbial example

SATs example

Insert **one** comma in the correct place in the sentence below.

Limping slightly the old man walked to the end of the road.

Limping slightly, the old man walked to the end of the road.

Embedded clause example

SATs example

Insert a **pair of commas** in the correct place in the sentence below.

I enjoy sitting in my bedroom even though it is quite small and listening to music.

I enjoy sitting in my bedroom, even though it is quite small, and listening to music.

Commas in a list example

SATs example

Add three **commas** in the correct places in the sentence below.

She wore a dark red skirt a woollen jumper a scarf with matching hat thick socks and black boots.

She wore a dark red skirt, a woollen jumper, a scarf with matching hat, thick socks and black boots.

Apostrophes for possession or contraction

Apostrophes can be used in two ways: to show contraction or to mark possession.

Contraction

An apostrophe may be used to show a contraction (see p. 22). This is where two words have been joined together and shortened. The apostrophe shows this joining and normally goes where a letter has been taken out or omitted. For example, don't, you've, haven't.

Possession

Apostrophes are also used to show possession or ownership. For example, Lucy's computer, Andrew's drink or the dog's ball.

Examples

Emma's bag was leather, and she didn't want to scratch it.

Emma owns the bag, so the apostrophe is used to show possession. 'Didn't' is a contraction of 'did not'.

This morning, Amelia's alarm clock went off early so she snoozed it. She'd have been better off just getting up.

The alarm clock is Amelia's possession; the apostrophe shows this. She'd is a contraction of 'she would'.

NINJA TIP:

If you are unsure whether an apostrophe is for contraction or possession, try to say the expanded form. With possession, there is none. For example 'Emma's house' is just Emma's house — there's no expanded form. The apostrophe shows that Emma owns the house.

SATs example

Circle the world in the passage that contains an **apostrophe** for **possession**.

It's five o'clock. Let's leave early and we'll be able to go to Emma's house first.

Emma's

SATs example

Insert an **apostrophe** in the correct place in the sentence below.

Pupils coats should be hung on the pegs.

Pupils'

NINJA TIP:
Watch out for plural possessive apostrophes! If the subject is plural, as in pupils, then the possessive apostrophe should be placed at the end of the word. For example: the dog's water bowl (one dog), the dogs' water bowl (more than one dog).

SATs example

Tick one box in each row to show whether the apostrophe is used for a **contracted form** or **possession**.

Sentence	Apostrophe for a contracted form	Apostrophe for possession
Where is Karen's pen?		
Joshua's hungry.		
Please get the dog's dinner.		
The cat's outside.		

Possession, contraction, possession, contraction

Speech punctuation/ inverted commas

Speech punctuation, known as inverted commas, is used to show where direct speech begins and ends.

Example

In these examples, the speech verbs are in bold, inverted commas are highlighted and any commas or internal punctuation are underlined.

"I want to visit the museum," **said** Freddy.

"Do you like vegetables?" **asked** Mrs Shepherd.

> **NINJA TIP:**
> When the inverted commas come before the speech verb, the comma remains inside the inverted commas.

> **NINJA TIP:**
> The comma comes after the speech verb and before the inverted commas when the speech verb comes before the direct speech.

Freddy **said**, "I would like to visit the museum."

Alexander and Thea **shouted**, "How slow are you guys!"

SATs example

Tick two boxes to show where the missing **inverted commas** should go.

☐   ☐☐   ☐
↓   ↓↓   ↓
Roman life was unlike modern life, the archaeologist said.

First box, second box

> **SATS TIP**
> If you have to write the comma yourself, ensure that it is placed in the correct position or you may lose the mark — even if your inverted commas are in the correct position.

SATs example

Rewrite the sentence below as **direct speech**.
Remember to punctuate your sentence correctly.

I asked her whether she needed any help.

I asked, _____

I asked, "Do you need any help?"

Colon/semi-colon

Colons
Colons separate two independent but linked clauses. Importantly, the second clause stresses, emphasises, adds clarification or adds further detail to the first clause.

> **SATS TIP**
> Colons can also be used to introduce a list. For example, Mia's shopping list included: eggs, milk and bread.

Example
I decided it was time to go home: it had started to snow heavily.

Semi-colons
Semi-colons can be used instead of or as an alternative to a co-ordinating conjunction when joining two independent or main clauses in a compound sentence.

> **NINJA TIP:**
> You don't need a capital letter after a colon or semi-colon is used.

Example
The cat ran through the bushes; the dog slept on the grass.

SATs example

Insert a **semi-colon** in the correct place in the sentence below.

Come and see me tomorrow I will not have time to see you today.

Come and see me tomorrow; I will not have time to see you today.

SATs example

Tick one box to show the correct place for a **colon** in the sentence below.

Tom needed to think carefully about his homework it looked very difficult.

Third box

SATs example

Insert a **colon** in the correct place in the sentence below.

Many fossils are not as big as people think some are so small that you need a microscope to see them.

Many fossils are not as big as people think: some are so small that you need a microscope to see them.

(Parenthesis)

Parenthesis refers to specific pieces of punctuation, used in pairs, to separate or enclose additional information. Parenthesis can come in the form of brackets, commas and dashes.

In the following examples, the underlined information is the additional information that is marked by the brackets, commas or dashes.

Brackets
This afternoon, Mr Roberts (aged 54) celebrated his birthday.

Commas
The church tower, St Augustine's Chapel, was measured at 347 feet tall.

Dashes
Upon discovering the sweets — all 43 glistening gems — the children immediately devoured them.

SATS TIP
The information in parenthesis isn't important to the structure of the sentence. So, if you read the sentence without it, it should still make sense.

SATs example

Insert a pair of **brackets** in the correct place in the sentence below.

The highest mountain in Great Britain is Ben Nevis 1,344 metres in Scotland.

(1,344 metres)

SATs example

Insert a **pair of dashes** in the correct place in the sentence below.

The Caspian Sea which is a saltwater lake is the largest inland body of water in the world.

— which is a saltwater lake —

Spelling

English grammar, punctuation and spelling: Paper 2

Test details

Test day - Monday (after the punctuation and grammar paper)

Time allowed - 20-30 minutes

Number of questions - 20 questions. Each question is worth one mark. 50 marks total.

The marks for this paper are combined with the marks for the grammar and punctuation paper to give a combined grammar, punctuation and spelling mark out of 70.

Layout and appearance

The spelling paper looks like this. When you open the booklet, you will find two pages, each with ten sentences on (for 20 in total). Each sentence will have a missing word – this is where you will write the spelling.

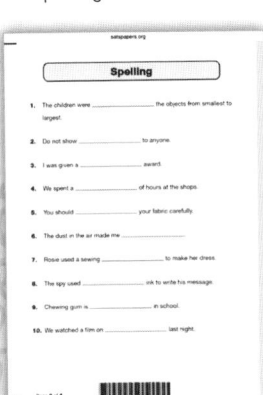

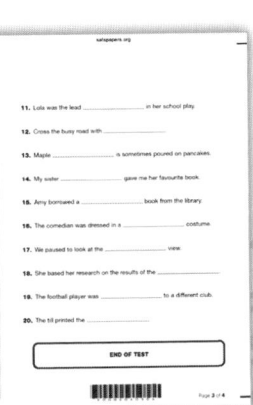

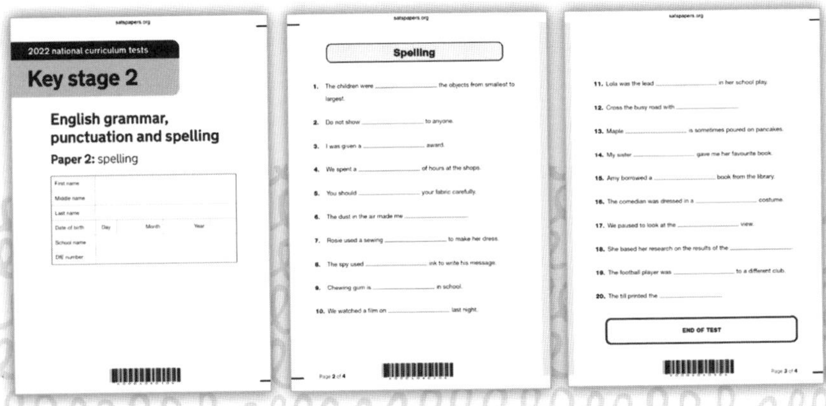

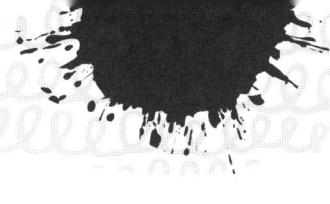

A teacher will read aloud the missing word that needs to be spelled, and then read the sentence with the word in it. Finally the teacher will repeat the word again.

Example questions

In the example below, the spelling is '**disrespect**'. The teacher will say, "The word is **disrespect**."

Then they will read the sentence aloud with the word in it. You need to spell 'disrespect' correctly on the line.

2. Do not show _____ to anyone.

In the example below, the spelling is '**invisible**'. The teacher will say, "The word is **invisible**."

Then they will read the sentence aloud with the word in it. You need to spell 'invisible' correctly on the line.

8. The spy used _____ ink to write his message.

NINJA TIP:
It's very important to write clearly. Try to print your letters. Sometimes joined-up writing can be confusing and can be marked wrong.

Tricky spelling rules to remember

The spelling test is all about preparation. Even if you are good at spellings, you can keep practising and get even better!

Here are some tricky spelling rules you can learn to help you.

1. i before e except after c (or when sounding like a)

- Remember this rhyme: 'i before e except after c,' or when sounding like a, as in 'neighbour' and 'weigh'.
- Examples: receive, deceive, ceiling
- Watch out for exceptions like 'science' and 'sufficient'!

2. Silent 'e' at the end of a word

- When a word ends with a silent 'e', it often makes the vowel before it say its name (long sound).
- Examples: kite, theme, bike

3. Doubling the final consonant before adding a suffix

- If a word ends in a single vowel followed by a single consonant, double the final consonant before adding '-ing,' '-ed,' or '-er'.
- Examples: run → running, hop → hopping
- Watch out for exceptions like start → starting

4. '-cial' and '-tial'

- If the last letter before 'shul' is a vowel, then use '-cial'. If the last letter is a consonant, use '-tial'.
- Examples: special, artifical, social, partial, essential, potential

5. Plural forms of words ending in 'y'

- If a word ends with 'y', change 'y' to 'i' and add 'es' to make it plural.
- Examples: baby → babies, city → cities
- Watch out for exceptions like day → days

6. Words with silent letters

- Some words have letters that you don't say out loud.
- Examples: knight, wrestle, subtle

7. Words ending in '-able' and '-ible'

- If you can add '-ing' to a word, use '-able'; otherwise, use '-ible.'
- Examples: legible, possible, reversible

8. Words with 'ough'

- The same letters can sound different in different words.
- Examples: though, through, thought, rough, cough

9. 'c' and 'k' sounds

- Use 'c' when followed by 'e,' 'i,' or 'y'; use 'k' in other cases.
- Examples: cat, kite, car
- Remember, there are some common exceptions like school and kit!

10. Words with multiple acceptable spellings

- Some words can be spelled in different ways, such as where, wear or were.
- Remember to listen to the whole sentence so you can work out which version of the spelling you should write down.

NINJA TIP: Practising these rules and reading regularly will help you become a spelling ninja!

Reading

English reading

Test details

Test day - Tuesday
Time allowed - 60 minutes (1 hour)
Number of questions - Approximately 35 questions. Questions can be worth one, two or three marks. 50 marks total..

Layout and appearance

The reading paper has two booklets. The first booklet is the texts. You will find three texts in the booklet. Normally the texts become increasingly difficult, so text three is more often the most challenging. Texts can be one, two or three pages long. Texts could be fiction, non-fiction or even poetry.

The second booklet of the reading test is the answer booklet, which looks like this:

NINJA TIP:
Double check each text. Don't assume that it is only one page, it might be two or even three pages long.

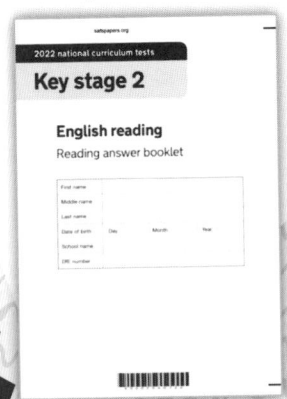

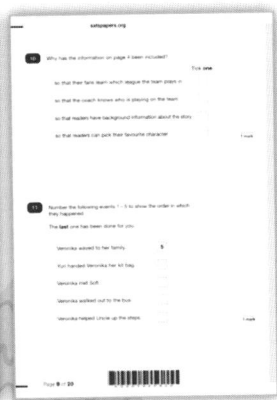

> **SATS TIP**
> The reading booklet is normally seven to nine page, so, there can be a lot to read.

Example questions

Question types can vary. Some questions want you write answers, others want you to tick boxes and some want you to order information with numbers.

SATs example

1 Veronika's football team has two names. What are the **two** names?

1. _____

2. _____

SATs example

22 Complete the table with facts from the text.

Age that Vladik is now:	
How long Vladik has been doing the routine:	
Age his daughter started walking:	
Age that Vladik started dance classes:	

SATs example

29 Look at the top of page 11.

Give **three** ways you can tell things have gone back to normal.

1. _____

2. _____

3. _____

NINJA TIP: Look out for the marks on the right-hand side of the page.

Pre-reading a text and finding key words

The first thing you need to do when reading a text in a SATs paper is to be ready to identify the key words or key information as you read it. But what is a 'key word' or 'key information'? Let's get specific.

Nouns (proper, common and abstract):
names, places, people, objects, items, emotions

Numbers:
numbers, dates, times, years, money, units of measure, fractions, percentages

Unknown vocabulary:
Highlight or underline any words you do not know. Just because you don't know what it means, it doesn't mean that you can't use it to answer questions.

> **NINJA TIP:**
> Proper nouns are easy to spot as they have capital letters, but common nouns can often be missed. Be sure to identify as many as you can when you pre-read a text.

From now on, whenever you read the phrase 'key words', it means the **nouns, numbers** and **unknown vocabulary** — it's very specific!

You can practise identifying key words or information by reading a text and highlighting or underlining these when you spot them. By highlighting the key words in the text, you can focus in on only the essential information.

Let's have a look at identifying the key words in a short extract. Even this short text might look tough, but we don't need all of the words in the text to answer questions effectively.

MICROBES

The five types of living microbes are bacteria, viruses, fungi, algae and protozoa. Microbes are microscopic, which means that they are so small that you would need a microscope to see them. They have existed for 3.5 billion years and are vital in sustaining life on our planet. Microbes can thrive in extreme environments where no other life forms could exist. Interestingly, most microbes don't cause disease; less than 5% do. Did you know that if you put all of the bacteria from a human's digestive system on a set of scales, they would weigh approximately 1 kilogram? That's the same as a bag of sugar! In one teaspoon of soil, there will be 1 billion bacteria, 120,000 fungi and 25,000 algae! When you cough, germs can travel about 3 metres if you do not cover your mouth and nose. Generally, there are between 10,000 and 10 million bacteria on each hand. Microbes are everywhere – they're on us, in us and around us.

As you read the text, highlight the key words or key information (nouns, numbers and unknown vocabulary).

NINJA TIP: Try to only highlight one or two words at a time.

MICROBES

The **five** types of **living microbes** are **bacteria, viruses, fungi, algae and protozoa**. Microbes are **microscopic**, which means that they are so small that you would need a **microscope** to see them. They have existed for **3.5 billion years** and are **vital** in **sustaining** life on our **planet**. Microbes can **thrive** in **extreme environments** where no other life forms could exist. Interestingly, most microbes **don't cause disease**, less than **5%** do. Did you know that if you put all of the bacteria from a **human's digestive system** on a set of scales, they would **weigh** approximately **1 kilogram**? That's the same as a **bag of sugar**! In **one teaspoon** of **soil**, there will be **1 billion bacteria**, **120,000 fungi** and **25,000 algae**! When you **cough**, **germs** can travel about **3 metres** if you do not cover your **mouth** and **nose**. Generally, there are between **10,000** and **10 million bacteria** on each **hand**. Microbes are everywhere – they're on us, in us and around us.

No two people will highlight all the same words, but if you identify most of them then you are in a great position to answer questions.

Here are two texts to practise highlighting, underlining or circling the key words or key information.

> **SATS TIP**
> Remember to look out for common nouns, they can be easily missed.

BIODEGRADABILITY (non-fiction)

In nature, different materials biodegrade at different rates. If an apple core is thrown into the bushes along with an aluminium drink can, the apple core will have disappeared in a few months but the can will remain largely the same. It may take 80-200 years before the can disappears entirely. It takes orange peel two to five weeks to decompose. A cardboard box would take 2 months, balloons 4 years, crisp packets 80 years, plastic bottles 450 years and a glass bottle 1 million years. A plastic bag will break down in 20 years but it doesn't actually *biodegrade*. It breaks down into smaller pieces of plastic known as 'microplastics'. These won't block up the stomachs of dolphins or whales, but they are toxic and build up in the food chain. We need to focus on reducing our use of products that take a long time to biodegrade completely.

THE TRENCH (fiction)

Private Anderson sat shivering in the trench. Memories of the day haunted his night. The shelling had been relentless. Boom! Boom! Boom! Hour after hour. A shell had gone off just next to the sandbags above his battalion's heads. He had crouched under his green, metallic Tommy helmet. But Private Smith had been struck by falling rocks. He was badly wounded. Private Smith, Paddy Smith, had been his best friend in school and lived in a house down the street. Their battalion was a 'Pal Battalion'; it was made up of friends, neighbours and even relatives. They had all known each other their entire lives. When one of them was injured, they all felt it. It could have been worse, he supposed.

Private Anderson shivered again. The duck boards that lined the floor were submerged in yellow, soupy water. When would the soldiers be home again and away from this?

> **NINJA TIP:**
> Fiction texts are likely to have far fewer numbers and statistics, so focus more on nouns and unknown vocabulary.

Skimming and scanning

Skimming and scanning is an important skill when it comes to reading. Essentially, your ability to skim and scan is your ability to locate the information you need as quickly and efficiently as possible.

When skimming and scanning, you need to move your eyes over a text to locate a specific piece of information, but you must apply a strategy to ensure that you find it easily. If you can skim and scan well, then you should be able to move from a whole text of information down to a specific sentence or even a word.

Once you have read a text, it's important to try to remember whether key information was in the beginning, middle or end of the text.

Skimming:
Moving from the whole text to the correct section or paragraph of a text.

Scanning:
Looking for specific key words after locating the correct paragraph or section.

Normally you would use skimming and scanning once you have read the text and you are answering questions, where you need to constantly be navigating the text to find answers. Check out the **Key words in the question strategy** (p. 61) to see how to use skimming and scanning to answer questions efficiently.

Develop your skimming and scanning skills with some of the activities on the next pages.

NINJA TIP:
You can use clues such as headings, subheadings, images and quotations to help you get to the correct area of the text.

Skimming and scanning: Images

Before you skim and scan a text, let's get your eyes moving around an image to spot and retrieve information. Can you find the following items in the image?

teacher	noticeboard	plant	clock	bin
blackboard	teacher's desk	chair	pencil	book

58

Skimming and scanning: Timetables

Information can be presented in many different ways – not just as an image or a piece of text. Infographics, tables and timetables are just some of the ways that information can be presented. Let's retrieve some information from the timetable below.

	5.00 pm		6.00 pm		7.00 pm	
BBC One	Pointless 5.15 pm		BBC News at Six 6.00 pm	BBC London 6.30 pm	The One Show 7.00 pm	EastEnders 7.30 pm
BBC Two	Flog It! 5.00 pm		Richard's House 6.00 pm	B&B by the Sea 6.30 pm	Live Snooker 7.00 pm	
ITV	The Chase 5.00 pm		ITV News London 6.00 pm	ITV Evening News 6.30 pm		Emmerdale 7.30 pm
Channel 4	Four in a bed 5.00 pm	Strangers on a plane 5.30 pm	The Simpsons 6.00 pm	Hollyoaks 6.30 pm	Channel 4 News 7.00 pm	
Channel 5	5 News at 5 5.00 pm		Eggheads 6.00 pm	Celebrity Eggheads 6.30 pm	Police Interceptors 7.00 pm	

Example questions

What time is *The Simpsons* being shown?
Which channel can you watch *Flog It* on?
Name three programmes being shown at 6.00 pm.
What time is *The Chase* on ITV?
B&B by the Sea is shown at what time?
Which channel is *Pointless* shown on?
Which programme is on BBC TWO at 7.00 pm?

SATS TIP
SATs reading papers often present information in tables or unfamiliar formats that don't involve much reading but do require you to retrieve information.

Skimming and scanning: Text

When it comes to a text, always read the text first before trying to answer any questions. Try to remember whether key information appears in the beginning, middle or end of the text.

Can you find these words in the text?

paralyse	venomous	dinosaurs	species	whale
stinging	brain	stun	eyes	smack

TEXT 1 (non-fiction)

Jellyfish have roamed the seas for at least 600 million years, even before the dinosaurs roamed the land! These incredible invertebrates have no brain, heart, bones or eyes. They use their stinging tentacles to stun or paralyse prey before eating it. The most venomous marine animal on earth is considered to be the Australian box jellyfish. A single sting can kill an adult human in just a few minutes. There are over 200 species of jellyfish and a group of jellyfish is called a 'bloom', 'swarm' or 'smack'. 95% of a jellyfish is water; human bodies are up to 60% water. The largest known species of jellyfish is the 'lion's mane jellyfish'. Also known as the 'hair jelly', the largest recorded specimen had tentacles around 37 m long — longer than a blue whale!

NINJA TIP:

If you are looking for a particular word, keep the first two letters of the word in your mind. Your brilliant brain can recognise words that you are reading from the first two letters. So, if you are looking for 'venomous', scan for 've'.

Can you find these words in the text?

sprout	prickled	merge	teeth	clouds
hunger	ripped	floor	flatter	shout

TEXT 2 (fiction)

He felt a hunger like never before. The full moon pushed aside the clouds and he looked up at it. A sudden pain prickled his skin. He let out a shout, but it was more of a howl. Hair began to sprout all over his body.

His mouth and nose began to merge into a snout. His teeth began to grow longer and pointed. Then his ears grew wider and flatter. All the while, the hair grew and grew. His clothes ripped and he fell to the floor. He was on all fours now, howling and howling up at the moon.

NINJA TIP:

As you read the text for the first time, underline with a pencil any words you do not know.

Key words in the question strategy

Once you can identify key words or key information in any text, you can start to use them to answer questions quickly and efficiently using the skimming and scanning technique (p. 57).

Step 1
Read the text. Highlight/identify the key words and information in the text (nouns, numbers or unknown vocabulary) using the skimming and scanning technique.

Step 2
Read the question and highlight any key words.

Step 3
Locate the key word/information from the question in the text.

Step 4
Once you find that word, go back to the beginning of that sentence and read the sentence in full. The answer should be here.

Step 5
If the answer isn't obvious, read the sentence before the key word and the sentence after.

> **SATS TIP**
> Sometimes, being able to identify a verb in the text and match it to the question can be really useful. For example, the word '**existed**' in the text on the next page stands out and is unlikely to be repeated, meaning that if it appears in a question, it should be very easy to locate quickly.

Key words in the question strategy

Apply the key words in the question strategy to this text.

MICROBES

The five types of living microbes are bacteria, viruses, fungi, algae and protozoa. Microbes are microscopic, which means that they are so small that you would need a microscope to see them. They have existed for 3.5 billion years and are vital in sustaining life on our planet. Microbes can thrive in extreme environments where no other life forms could exist. Interestingly, most microbes don't cause disease, less than 5% do. Did you know that if you put all of the bacteria from a human's digestive system on a set of scales, they would weigh approximately 1 kilogram? That's the same as a bag of sugar! In one teaspoon of soil, there will be 1 billion bacteria, 120,000 fungi and 25,000 algae! When you cough, germs can travel about 3 metres if you do not cover your mouth and nose. Generally, there are between 10,000 and 10 million bacteria on each hand. Microbes are everywhere – they're on us, in us and around us.

Example questions

How far can germs travel when you cough?

In this question, look to find the key words 'cough' or 'germ' in the text, then read around it to find the answer. The answer is 'about 3 metres'.

Name five types of living microbes.

In this question, look for the key words 'living microbes' and read on to find the five answers: 'bacteria, viruses, fungi, algae and protozoa'.

NINJA TIP: The answers above are great examples of unknown vocabulary. You don't need to know or understand what these words mean to answer the question.

Where would you find 1 billion bacteria?

In this question, it is very unlikely that '1 billion' would be repeated in the text, so if you can locate '1 billion' (a number) and read the sentence it is found in, you should find the answer. The answer is 'soil'.

Retrieval

These types of questions require you to retrieve information and to write a clear answer in the space provided.

Use the key words in the question strategy (nouns, numbers and unknown vocabulary) to locate the information you need in the text.

INCREDIBLE HUMAN BODY

The human body is incredible and full of fascinating facts. Did you know that the average person has 67 different species of bacteria in their belly button? Skin is the body's biggest organ and we lose about 4 kg of skin cells every year. The human heart beats more than three billion times in an average lifespan. Your eyes blink approximately 20 times a minute, that's over ten million times a year! Humans are not the strongest, biggest or fastest animals on Earth but we *are* the best at long-distance running – Sir Mo Farah is the perfect example. Our upright posture, long legs and ability to sweat (and therefore shed heat) are all factors that make us good runners. Your body has more than 600 muscles. The strongest muscle is located in the jaw and known as the masseter muscle. The stapedius muscle, in the middle of the ear, is the weakest.

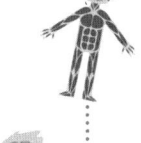

Example questions

How many different species of bacteria are found in the belly button? _____

What do we lose 4 kg of every year? _____

Where is the strongest muscle located? _____

Which muscle is the weakest? _____

Who is the perfect example of a long-distance runner? _____

How many times does a heart beat in an average lifespan? _____

What is the body's biggest organ? _____

How many times does an eye blink, on average, every minute? _____

SATS TIP — Be sure to write your answer clearly so that it can be read and understood. Answers could range from a single word to a full sentence.

True or false questions

True or false question ask you to put a tick in the true box or the false box.

To answer these questions, first read the text using the skimming and scanning technique. Then read the statement, find the key words in the statement and go back to that part of the text to reread and check whether the statement is true or false.

ANGLO-SAXON LAW

Around AD 1000, the Anglo-Saxons did have laws, but they were quite different from the laws we have today. The Saxons operated a system called 'weregild' for crimes against people – if a person injured another, they had to pay for the harm caused. If a person killed someone, they paid money to the dead person's family. The weregild payable for the murder of an Anglo-Saxon thane (head man of a community) was 6,000 pennies, the weregild for a king was 90,000.

There were no prisons, so anyone found guilty of a crime was either fined, tortured or executed, depending on the severity of their crime. If you injured a person, fines could range from 200 to 1,200 shillings. For breaking into someone's house, the fine was five shillings, paid directly to the home-owner. Crimes that were considered less significant, like stealing – or if you couldn't afford a fine – could involve a finger, nose, hand, foot or big toe being chopped off. For more grievous crimes, like murder or being a traitor, the punishment was death.

NINJA TIP: Lots of pupils think true or false questions is a guessing activity. It isn't. Use key words to go back to the text and work out whether the statement is true or false.

SATs example

Sentence	True	False
In AD 1000, Anglo-Saxons had no laws.		
Fines for breaking into homes were paid to the king.		
You would go to jail if you couldn't afford a fine.		
Anglo-Saxon laws were similar to the laws we have today.		
The Saxons operated a system called 'weregild' for crimes against people.		
People who stole could have their nose cut off.		

false, false, false, false, true, true

Find and copy questions

Use the key words in the question strategy (nouns, numbers and unknown vocabulary) to locate the information you need in the text.

GRENDEL

Beowulf held his sword, Hrunting, tightly in his hands. His brow furrowed and beads of sweat formed on his brow. He heard the heavy footsteps and growling from outside of the Mead Hall. Grendel was coming. The demon from below the earth was on its way, stalking towards King Hrothgar's Hall of Heorot.

Beowulf's soldiers were nervous. There were 15 of them and they all knew they would be no match for the demon. It suddenly burst through the huge wooden doors. Beowulf and his soldiers stood defiant and ready for battle. Grendel roared with fury that anybody dared to challenge it.

The soldiers bellowed a war cry back at the beast and ran with swords swinging. They chopped and hacked but nothing could pierce Grendel's armour-plated skin. Beowulf would have to use his strength. He threw Hrunting to the ground and grabbed the demon with bare hands.

Example questions

1) Write the word from the text that tells us the soldiers shouted loudly.

_____

2) Write the word that suggests that Grendel had been creeping up on the Mead Hall.

_____

3) Write the word that suggests the doors of the Mead Hall were damaged badly.

_____

bellowed, stalking, burst

Multiple choice questions

Use the key words in the question strategy (nouns, numbers and unknown vocabulary) to locate the information you need in the text.

THE ALLIANCE

The city was bustling with activity. Vast screens lit up every building with vivid colours advertising the latest products to buy. Swift vehicles flew past these in endless lines hurrying here and there. Hovercams made announcements constantly. The noise was incredible.

Down below, the streets had roads with automated vehicles. Pedestrians used travellators. The city was in constant movement.

Vast, domed skyscrapers dominated the landscape. There were electronic signs and wall screens on every surface. Behind these, people lived with their robotic helpers. Drones were sent out of open windows to deliver packages or pick up parcels of supplies.

The spaceport was at the edge of the city. Huge spaceships came and went. There was a wormhole just beyond the Moon and interstellar travel was a daily occurrence. Earth was now part of an intergalactic alliance.

SATs example

Circle the correct option to complete each sentence below.

1 What lit up the buildings with vivid colours? Circle the correct answer.

- huge streetlights
- vast screens
- flying car headlights
- flashing machines

2 What piece of equipment were pedestrians using? Circle the correct answer.

- hoverboards
- flying cars
- robots
- travellators

vast screens, travellators

SATs example

3 Where was the spaceport? Circle the correct answer.

- hovering above the city
- in the upper atmosphere
- the edge of the city
- at the heart of the city

4 What was just beyond the Moon? Circle the correct answer.

- the rest of the galaxy
- a black hole
- a super nova
- a wormhole

5 What were used to deliver and collect parcels? Circle the correct answer.

- drones
- robots
- hover delivery machines
- underground tubes

the edge of the city, a wormhole, drones

SATS TIP
Remember to circle the answer as requested by the question. If you don't, you won't get the mark.

Sequencing

Sequencing questions ask you to show the order that information occurs in the text or the order in which something happened.

To answer sequencing questions, you can use shapes to help you order the information. Sequencing can seem tricky but this simple strategy can help you master this skill.

Step 1
Look at the question. Give each statement or word a symbol.

Step 2
Use key words in the statements to locate the information in the main text.

Step 3
When you find a specific piece of information, put the symbol linked to that information on the first word of that sentence. If you are just looking for a specific word or number, put the symbol exactly on that word.

Step 4
Place all of the symbols across the text. You can now easily see the order!

Circle is 1, Star is 2, Plus is 3, Triangle is 4 and Square is 5.

Step 5
Add the numbers into the original question.

SATS TIP
Use the key words in the questions (nouns, numbers and unknown vocabulary) to locate the information you need in the text.

Sequencing

THE INUIT

The early Inuit settlers made their home in the far frozen north of North America, adapting their life to the frozen land and sea of the arctic. They learned to construct warm homes out of snow and ice for the winter. During the summer, they made homes from animal skin stretched over a frame made from whalebones or driftwood. The Inuit word for home is 'igloo'. Traditionally, the Inuit obtained the majority of their food by fishing and hunting reindeer, seal, walrus and whale meat. Nowadays, there are around 150,000 Inuit people in the world. Most live in Alaska, but there are also Inuit in Greenland, Canada and Siberia. One of the most important Inuit festivals is nalukataq, or the 'spring whaling festival'. This feast is held to appease the spirits of whales killed in hunting. The festival involves members of the community being tossed into the air from a walrus-skin!

SATs example

1 Number the statements 1–5 to show the order they occur in the text.

made from whalebones or driftwood ★	
Most live in Alaska ●	
early Inuit settlers ✚	
Inuit festivals is nalukataq ▲	
construct warm homes ■	

3, 4, 1, 5, 2

Sequencing (fiction)

WATER HOLE WAR

The hippopotamus got to his feet. Another male was approaching the water hole and he had to defend his territory. There just wasn't enough room here for them both. The dry season was the worst it had ever been. The temperature was incredibly high and the water hole was nearly all dry.

The hippopotamus ran towards the other male. This hippo's mouth was open, with teeth bared ready for a fight. The two huge animals slammed into one another. They snapped their massive jaws and rammed their heads together.

The imposter was smaller and younger. He soon gave up and ran away to a safe distance. The victorious hippo sank down into the warm mud. He had won the battle but more hippos were gathering. Their home was disappearing and it was about to get worse. Climate change was affecting every animal on the planet.

SATs example

2 Number the words 1–5 to show the order they occur in the text.

imposter	☐
territory	☐
disappearing	☐
rammed	☐
victorious	☐

3, 1, 5, 2, 4

Sequencing (non-fiction)

PERCY SHAW

Percy Shaw OBE was born in Halifax on 15 April 1890. Growing up, he enjoyed mechanical tinkering with motorcycles and cars. His ability to repair these led him to eventually inventing his 'cat's eyes'. An encounter with a cat one foggy night was his inspiration! In the 1930s, motorists relied upon the reflections of their headlights from the tramlines to get them safely home at night. When trams ceased to be used, the tramlines were removed, depriving the motorist of this aid.

Driving home on that foggy night, Shaw noticed the reflection of his headlights in the eyes of the cat. He also realised he was travelling down the wrong side of the road and would have plummeted over the edge had he continued! Inspired to make the roads safe again, Shaw developed his Catseye Reflecting Roadstuds. Shaw's inventive mind and determination enabled him to illuminate the roads at night once more.

SATs example

3 Number the facts 1–5 to show the order they occur in the text.

enjoyed mechanical tinkering with motorcycles and cars	
plummeted over the edge	
illuminate the roads at night	
born in Halifax	
reflection of his headlights in the eyes of the cat	

2, 4, 5, 1, 3

Inference: Images

Inference is the process of making sense of the information we read or see and making logical conclusions based on the evidence we have. Inference never says things directly, but offers clues to let you know more about the character, situation or idea.

Before we look at words and texts, let's make some basic inferences about the faces below based on the evidence you have and your knowledge about the world.

This face is smiling and their eyes are wide, so we can infer they are happy. The image doesn't have a label saying that they are happy, but we can make this inference from the simple clues.

Their eyes are down and their eyebrows make a frown, so we can infer they are upset or sad.

Their eyes are nearly closed and we can see bags under them, so we can infer they are tired.

Their eyebrows are angled and their teeth are showing, so we can infer they are angry.

Inference: Images

Let's have a look at another example of inference. Imagine the question is asking you: 'What can we infer about the people who own these shoes?'

You could infer that this person works in an office or a professional job that requires then to wear trousers, suit and smart shoes..

You could infer that this person is a builder or someone who works in an environment where they need a hard-wearing and tough boot. They could be a builder, farmer or tradesperson.

You could infer that this person is relaxing, maybe even on holiday.

You could infer that this person enjoys running or playing sport.

NINJA TIP:

The more information we have, the better our inference would be. For example, if all of the shoes above had another item next to them that was a clue about the person, we would be able to make an even more precise inference.

Inference: Thoughts

Inference questions often ask you to infer what a character's actions and words might imply, so you can work out what they are thinking.

Look at the example below. As you read the extract, try to spot the clues as you read. Look out for them in bold. As we are reading, we need to be aware and build an understanding that she is upset, but she is trying not to show it.

If we pick up on these clues as we read, answering the question below is pretty simple.

> 'It's the Youth Club... they've closed it.' Everyone one was silent, barely taking a breath. Robbie and Andros glanced at each other, and then to Robbie's dad, before quickly looking away. All the colour in his face had faded away, his mouth had fallen open. His eyes were still fixed on the message his phone, his eyes clearly filling with tears. 'Close the Youthy!' Andros muttered angrily. 'How can they do that? It's there for everyone!' 'Yup, it's everyone's favourite place to go!' Robbie agreed. 'You boys better get off to your football match, or you'll be on the bench,' said Dad. His voice sounded different, smaller somehow. 'But, we need to...' Andros started to say. 'I'll take care of that, you just concentrate on your match.' Dad gave the boys a nod and wink, but it wasn't with his normal confidence. If he was trying to make the boys feel better, it wasn't helping.

SATs example

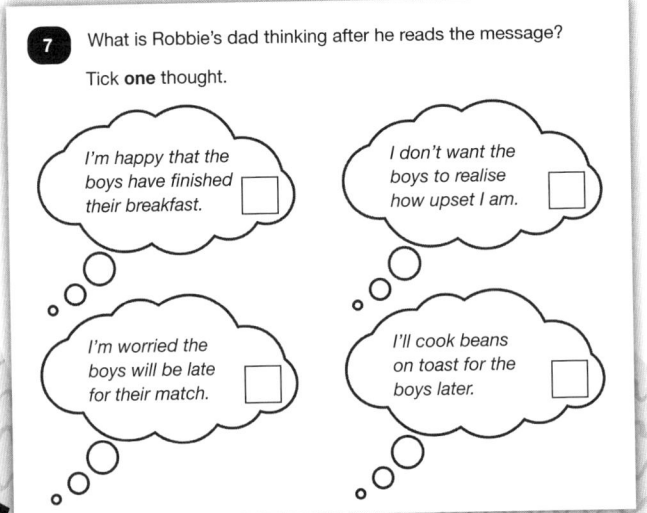

7 What is Robbie's dad thinking after he reads the message?

Tick **one** thought.

- I'm happy that the boys have finished their breakfast.
- I don't want the boys to realise how upset I am.
- I'm worried the boys will be late for their match.
- I'll cook beans on toast for the boys later.

NINJA TIP:

SATs question can often be presented in strange ways. In this example, the thought clouds represent what the character is thinking.

I don't want the boys to realise how upset I am.

Inference: Explain

A huge clue that you are answering an inference question is the fact that the question will ask you to explain. It might also ask you to provide evidence.

> Maria led Oliver across the tangled ground to the hidden monument. It was a column of marble, weathered and mossy with age. A delicate crown sat at the top, and an inscription was carved into a flat slab at the base. Oliver used his thumbnail to scrape out the letters that were cut into it. It was a name.
>
> Maria's family name.

SATs example

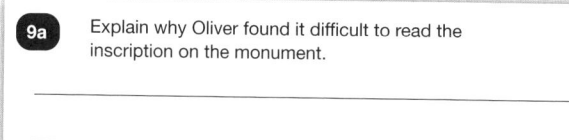

9a Explain why Oliver found it difficult to read the inscription on the monument.

it is mossy / dirty, it is covered, or it is weathered

NINJA TIP:
Inference is like being a detective. You need to pick up the clues as you read, and understand what they are telling you indirectly.

SATS TIP
Look out for the word 'explain' in questions. If you see 'explain', it's probably an inference-style question.

Inference: What does it suggest?

Another way you can identify an inference question is to spot the phrase 'What does it suggest?'. All this is asking is what are the clues telling you? What does this tell you?

Let's look at an example.

> We slowly and cautiously set forth into the unknown. After a few hundred yards of thick forest, we entered a region where the stream widened out and formed a considerable bog. High reeds grew thickly before us, with tree-ferns scattered amongst them, all of them swaying in a brisk wind. Suddenly Lord John, who was walking first, halted.

SATs example

27 How does the first paragraph suggest that the characters are in a 'lost world'?

_____

_____

It is referred to as 'the unknown', or they entered cautiously

76

Two- and three-mark questions: Using evidence to support

Inference questions can offer a lot of marks. This example has three marks available. It asks you to **explain**, which is a big clue that you need to make inferences.

This question wants you to give evidence too. This basically means prove it! Copy information from the text to support your answer.

> The tiny island, thick with creeping vines and roots, looked as if it floated. At its centre, an ancient oak tree towered over it. The tree's branches were like bent fingers, twisting and stretching outwards, until the tips of its leaves touched the still water. Oliver carefully steered the boat through a narrow opening in the branches. Then they stepped out of the boat, and into a murky green space under an umbrella of leaves. The air was cool and damp. Maria led Oliver across the tangled ground to the hidden monument. It was a column of marble, weathered and mossy with age. A delicate crown sat at the top, and an inscription was carved into a flat slab at the base. Oliver used his thumbnail to scrape out the letters that were cut into it.

SATs example

6 What impressions of the island do you get from these two paragraphs? Give **two**.

1. _____
2. _____

Reference any two of the following: uninhabited/abandoned; holds secrets; overgrown; dark/shady/gloomy; small; mysterious/creepy/unsettling; quiet/peaceful; important/a special place; old

NINJA TIP:
There are lots of different ways to answer these questions. You can still get one or two marks by just providing an answer to the question, even if you can't find the evidence to support your answer.

77

Two- and three-mark questions: Using evidence to support

Encounter in the Meadow

Miriam is a young forester. She often takes out her quad bike, 'Dusty', for a day of exploring the woods and animal spotting.

For the first time in over a fortnight, Miriam hadn't seen a deer all day. She was further from the farm than she had ever been, in over 14 acres of woodland. Dusty threw up a translucent mist of dried, mud track into the air behind her, and the bata-bata-bata of the engine was lost in the vast, emptiness and silence of the morning.

Miriam turned off the engine and rolled silently to a stop. She rummaged through her satchel to locate a flask of hot cocoa to warm her hands and her heart. As she poured the cocoa, chocolatey steam danced as it ascended, while delicately scented waves rose in front of her hazel eyes, stealing her attention away from the idyllic morning landscape. She sipped the drink slowly, savouring its delightful warmth.

Ssnffftt... Ssnffftt! The sound came from behind her, in the distance, and made her turn her head ever so slowly, careful not to make a sound.

Sssnnnnnfffftttt... Louder and longer, even closer now. Closer still... until...

Miriam gathered her courage and looked up.

A brown shape, much larger than the biggest deer, showed about five metres from the quad, obscured by the trees. It was like a tree but not, with a lion's mane. On its rounded head were stakes like tree branches, bigger than a man's outstretched arms, with sharpened tips at the end. As Miriam watched, astonished, the branches rose from the ground, and emerged from the cover of the trees into the peaceful meadow.

A buck! Its majestic head and antlers! That's what she had seen.

SATs example

1 How is the buck made to seem mysterious?
Explain **three** ways, giving evidence from the text to support your answer.

1. _____
2. _____
3. _____

Example answers: The text uses the mist from the hot chocolate to seem spooky; The unfamiliar sound the buck makes 'Sssnnnffftt'; It uses familiar things to describe the unrecognisable, for example how the antlers are described as branches at first.

'What impression' questions

'What impression' questions are very common questions in the reading paper. They are often worth three marks. When the question asks 'What impression', it is asking you 'What is your idea, feeling or opinion about someone or something?'

The 'What impression' question is really an inference question where you need to use evidence to support your opinion.

NINJA TIP:
Your impression is often very simple, don't overcomplicate it. For example, your impression of someone might be 'They are shy' or 'They are brave'. Simple!

> Jeremy heard a loud explosion and a red flash of light, but he held strong, not backing away. In the distance, he was sure he could hear a cry for help. He took a step closer to the whimpering sound.

SATs example

1. What impression do you get of Jeremy? Give one impression using two pieces of evidence to support your answer.

1. _____
2. _____

From the text, you might feel that Jeremy was brave. So, your impression of Jeremy is that he is brave. You need evidence to support your impression. Look again at the text:

Jeremy heard a loud explosion and a red flash of light, but he held strong, not backing away. In the distance, he was sure he could hear a cry for help. He took a step closer to the whimpering sound.

So, your impression is: Jeremy is brave.

Evidence 1: he held strong, not backing away

Evidence 2: he took a step closer

SATS TIP
This question is not asking you to explain, so be very precise and copy the evidence directly from the text.

'What impression' questions

Let's look at some other examples and how we might answer them.

As Evelyn approached the house from the rusted, wrought-iron gate, she ran fast, the once-grand residence looming larger with each step. The early morning breeze bullied its way through an overgrown garden, and a gentle sun provided some relief from the chilling wind. Grains of dust danced in the air, occasionally stinging her eyes as she neared the weather-worn structure. She stopped and scanned the house. A pair of stone lions who once guarded the entrance doors were now crumbling, and many tiles were missing from the roof. Some had fallen and hit the lions.

Evelyn hesitated briefly before summoning the courage go inside. Peeking through a window, she saw a sad scene - a room filled with neglected, dusty ornaments and damp, rotten furniture.

SATs example

32 What impressions do you get of Evelyn's house?

Give **two** impressions, using evidence from the text to support your answer.

Impression	Evidence

In this example, you need to give two impressions from reading the text and provide a piece of evidence for each impression.

Impression	Evidence
Impression 1: The house is old.	The stone lions were crumbling and many roof tiles were missing.
Impression 2: No one lived in the house.	Neglected ornaments and damp, rotten furniture.

'What impression' questions

John snuck into the kitchen and began to make a sandwich, even though he had been told that sneaking food was forbidden. The young boy was so hungry that the powers of hearing seemed to leave him. As he devoured the sandwich, Mrs Eldridge slipped into the room without John realising. As he chewed the final morsels, her eyes became enraged, unwavering from the now not-so-hungry boy. Before John had a chance to turn and realise that he was being stalked by the housekeeper, she slammed her fist down onto the worktop.

SATs example

38 Look at page 10.

What impressions do you get of Mrs Eldridge at this point in the extract?

Give **two** impressions, using evidence from the text to support your answer.

Impression	Evidence

In this example, we need to give two impressions from reading the texts and provide a piece of evidence for each impression.

Impression	Evidence
Impression 1: Mrs Eldridge was sneaky.	Mrs Eldridge slipped into the room without John realising.
Impression 2: Mrs Eldridge was angry.	Her eyes became enraged.

SATS TIP
This question is not asking you to explain, so be very exact with your evidence and copy the wording directly from the text.

'What impression' questions

Let's look at some other examples and how we might answer them.

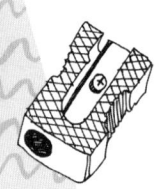

> Rain was lashing down from above the trees as Rita made her way along the riverbank. The sun had long since set and darkness had engulfed the countryside. Only a parade of lights, running parallel to the riverbank, lit Rita's path as she made her way towards the shelter of the local inn. As she turned a bend, each riverbank light suddenly darkened, one after the other, leaving Rita in the shadows. Although in complete darkness, she could sense the presence of someone now stood maybe a few metres ahead of her. Just then, a voice murmured to her, 'You must continue your journey; never give up.' As the last word was spoken, each light quickly illuminated to reveal that she was now alone again. She looked around, unflustered and composed, ready to continue her journey.

SATs example

33 Think about the whole text.

What impressions do you get of Rita as the narrator describes her unusual experience?

Give **two** impressions, using evidence from the text to support your answer.

1. _____

2. _____

In this example, we need to give two impressions from reading the text and provide a piece of evidence for each impression.

This is the same sort of question as the other examples you've seen, but this time you will need to write a full sentence that explains your impressions and the evidence that supports your impressions.

Impression 1 and evidence 1: Rita is brave because she is travelling alone at night, in the dark.

Impression 2 and evidence 2: Rita is calm because she is unflustered and remained composed when the lights went out and she was spoken to.

> **SATS TIP**
> The word 'because' can be helpful when answering this question.

Maths

Mathematics: Paper 1 arithmetic

Test details

Test day - Wednesday

Time allowed - 30 minutes

Number of questions - 36 questions. 32 questions are one mark; four questions are two marks. 40 marks in total.

The marks for this paper are combined with the marks for the two reasoning papers to give a combined mathematics mark out of 110.

Layout and appearance

The arithmetic paper looks like this. Most pages have three questions.

Example questions

All arithmetic questions look fairly similar.

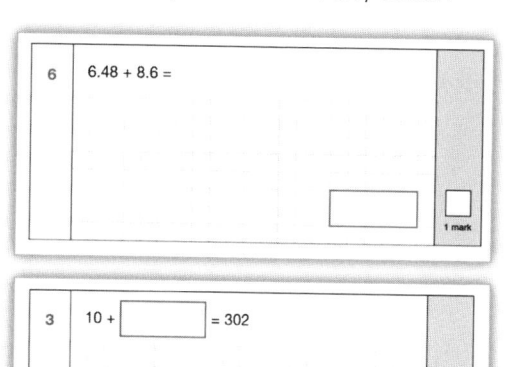

6	6.48 + 8.6 =

1 mark

3	10 + ☐ = 302

1 mark

SATS TIP
It is very important that you put the answer in the box provided in the question. If you don't write the answer in the box, you won't get a mark.

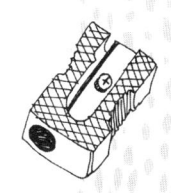

Long division questions and long multiplication questions are worth two marks each. Quite often these questions leave a little bit of extra blank space below them for you to work in, should you need it.

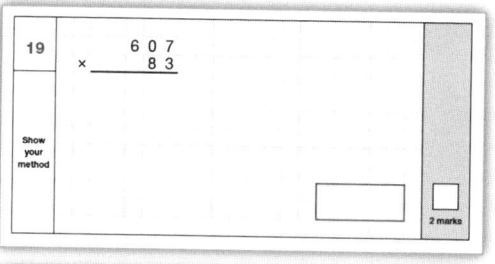

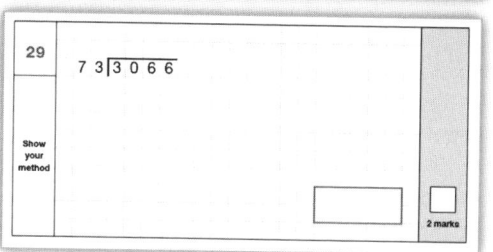

19	607 × 83
Show your method	

2 marks

29	7 3 ⟌ 3 0 6 6
Show your method	

2 marks

NINJA TIP:
Watch out for these two-mark questions. There are four in total, and they are usually near the end of the paper. Don't run out of time and miss them out!

Addition

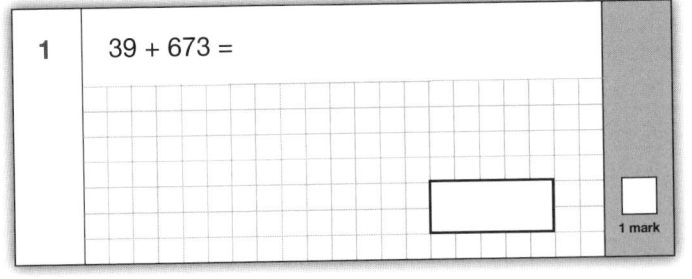

An addition problem is made up of two addends that equal the sum. The two addends will be smaller numbers than the sum; the sum is larger, as it is a combination of the two smaller numbers. You can usually use column addition to solve addition questions.

Step 1

Add the ones column; write the answer below.

```
  T O
  3 4
+ 2 5
-----
    9
```

Step 2

Add the tens column; write the answer below.

```
  T O
  3 4
+ 2 5
-----
  5 9
```

SATs example

1. 39 + 673 =

   1 mark

How to solve it

This is how we expect to see an addition problem in the SATs paper. Use column addition as a written method or mentally add 39 to 673.

NINJA TIP: In this instance, you could round 39 to 40, add 40 to 673, then take 1 away (mentally accurate and quick).

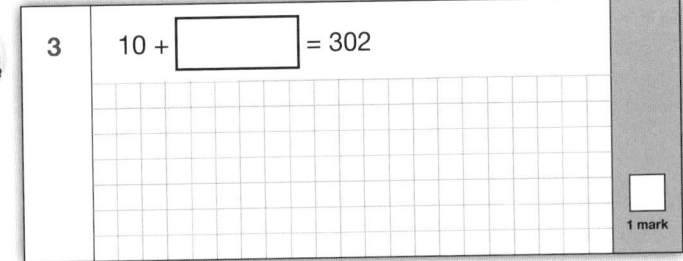

SATs example

3. 10 + ☐ = 302

   1 mark

How to solve it

What is missing? An addend! The sum is given (302). So, you need to find a smaller number – the missing addend. We must subtract the addend we do know from the sum. In this case, 302 - 10 = 292. You can do this in your head or use column subtraction (see p. 88).

SATs example

5   [ ] + 70 = 485

1 mark

How to solve it

Notice how you already have the sum (answer) in 485. If you remember that both of your addends equal the sum, then you know you must be looking for a smaller number. You need to subtract 70 from 485. You can do this in your head or use column subtraction (see p. 88).

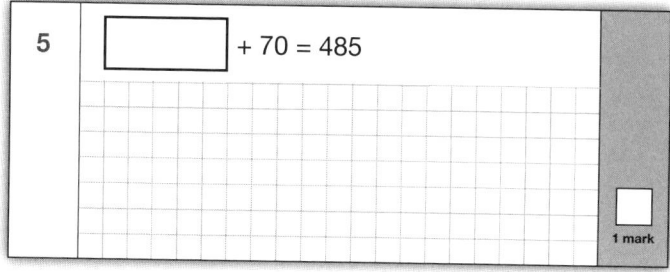

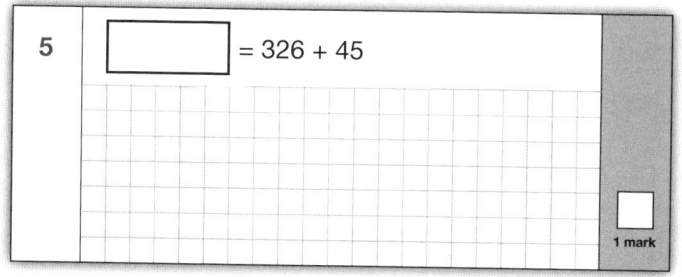

SATs example

5   [ ] = 326 + 45

1 mark

How to solve it

The key thing to notice is that you are missing the sum. So, quite simply, you just need to add together the two addends as normal. It's essentially the same as the first example, just laid out differently.

NINJA TIP:
Think of it this way. If you have the sum and are missing an addend, you need to subtract to find the missing addend.

SATS TIP
Addition may seem easy, but it's also easy to make silly mistakes. Sometimes doing a column addition or subtraction may take a little longer but will guarantee you get the right answer.

Practice TASK

1) 343 + 75 = ____
2) ____ + 49 = 370
3) 40 + ____ = 410
4) 87 = ____ + 34
5) 554 + 345 = ____

1) 418 2) 321 3) 370 4) 53 5) 899

Subtraction

A subtraction problem is made up of the **minuend** (the number being subtracted from – the larger number), the **subtrahend** (the number being taken away) and the **difference**, which you would normally call the answer. Referring to the answer as the difference will help you a lot. You can usually use column subtraction to solve subtraction questions.

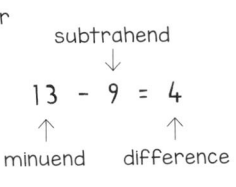

$$\underset{\uparrow}{13} - \underset{\uparrow}{9} = \underset{\uparrow}{4}$$
minuend subtrahend difference

NINJA TIP:
Think of subtraction problems as just finding the difference. For example, 13 - 9 = _____ is asking what the difference is between 9 and 13. Count on from 9 to 13; the difference is 4.

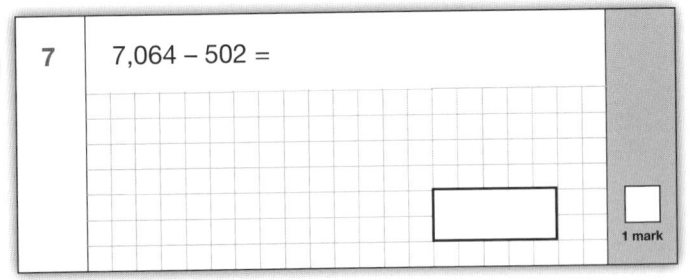

```
  1 3
-   9
-----
    4
```

SATs example

7 7,064 − 502 =

1 mark

How to solve it

This representation is how we expect to see a subtraction problem calculated. Use column subtraction as a written method.

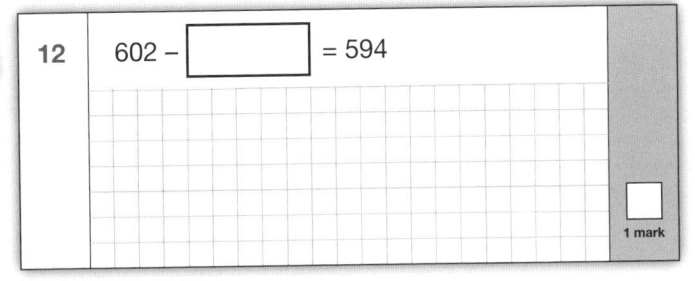

SATs example

12 602 − ☐ = 594

1 mark

How to solve it

Notice that you already have the difference. The subtrahend is missing; the subtrahend is smaller than the minuend. To find a smaller number, we must subtract: 602 - 594. In this instance, you could mentally count on from 594 to 602; it's 8.

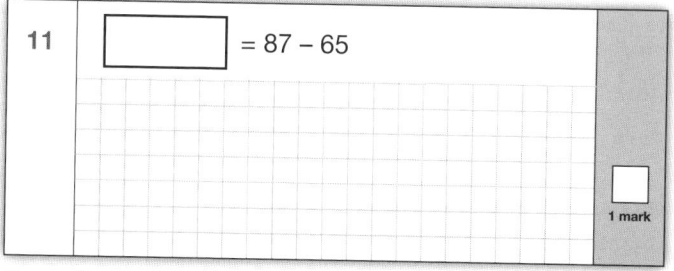

SATs example 10   ☐ − 10 = 298

1 mark

How to solve it

The minuend is missing. Remember, in a subtraction, the minuend is the largest number. So, in this problem, you need to add the two other numbers together: 298 + 10. Use column addition or calculate mentally in your head. The answer is 308.

SATs example 11   ☐ = 87 − 65

1 mark

How to solve it

In this problem, the difference is missing. It's a normal subtraction, just presented differently. Use column subtraction or calculate the difference in your head to work out 87 − 65. The difference is 22.

NINJA TIP:
In this problem, you could count on from 65 by adding 20 to get to 85, then adding 2 more to get to 87.

Practice TASK

1) 63 − 25 = ____
2) 87 − 54 = ____
3) 324 − ____ = 304
4) ____ = 68 − 43
5) ____ − 74 = 143

1) 38   2) 33   3) 20   4) 25   5) 217

Place value missing number

SATs example

15   3,050,020 = 3,000,000 + ☐ + 20

1 mark

Explanation

These questions are testing your knowledge of place value (ones, tens, hundreds, thousands, etc.) and only require you to write in the correct missing number in the expanded form, showing your understanding of the value of each digit.

How to solve it

Look at this example. Each digit represents a specific value, depending on the column it is placed in.

   7,635

There are 7 thousands (7,000), 6 hundreds (600), 3 tens (30) and 5 ones (5).

Th	H	T	O
7	6	3	5

7,000 + 600 + 30 + 5 = 7,635

NINJA TIP: Write the place value above the number, starting at the ones, tens, hundreds, etc. as you move from right to left.

Practice TASK

1) 457 = 400 + ____ + 7

2) 73,356 = 70,000 + ____ + 300 + 50 + 6

3) 457,005 = 400,000 + ____ + 7,000 + 5

1) 50 2) 3,000 3) 50,000

Short division

SATs example

11) $270 \div 3 =$

[ ] 1 mark

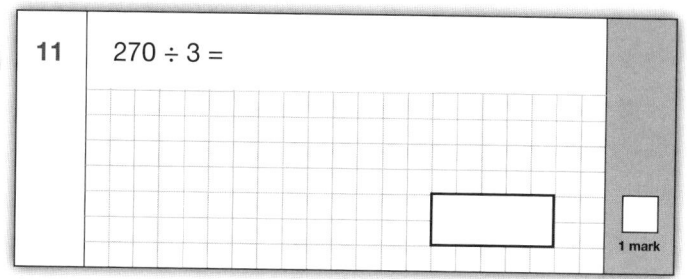

Explanation

Simple division problems have a **dividend** (the larger number being divided) and a **divisor** (the number we are dividing by). The answer is the **quotient**. In $270 \div 3$, we are essentially dividing 270 into 3 parts, or finding out how many 3s are in 270.

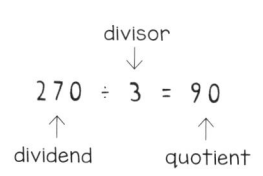

$$270 \div 3 = 90$$

↑ divisor above 3, ↑ dividend below 270, ↑ quotient below 90

SATS TIP
Short division is best used when dividing by one digit. If you are dividing by a two-digit number, you would use long division strategies (see p. 118).

How to solve it

Short division

Short division (sometimes called the bus stop method) is the most common written method. Here's an example.

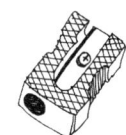

$840 \div 5 = ?$

Step 1: Write the question out as follows.

$5 \overline{)840}$

Step 2: How many 5s are in 8? 1, with 3 remainders.

$5 \overline{)8\,^34\,0}$ (with 1 above)

Step 3: How many 5s are in 34? 6, with 4 remainders.

$5 \overline{)8\,^34\,^40}$ (with 16 above)

Step 4: How many 5s are in 40? 8, with no remainders.

$5 \overline{)8\,^34\,^40}$ (with 168 above)

Using related facts

You can use 'related facts' (your knowledge of your times tables) to help you solve problems like this mentally. For example:

$$270 \div 3 = ?$$

$$27 \div 3 = 9$$

270 is 10 times larger than 27. If you make 9 10 times larger too, you get 90.

So the answer is 90.

$$231 \div 7 = ?$$

$21 \div 7 = 3$, so $210 \div 7$ must be 30.

This leaves 21. $21 \div 7 = 3$.

So the answer is 33.

NINJA TIP:
Watch out for questions where the quotient or answer is missing, but it is shown first in the question. Don't worry, just answer as normal. For example: ____ = 231 ÷ 7

Practice TASK

1) 240 ÷ 4 = ____
2) 560 ÷ 8 = ____
3) 270 ÷ 6 = ____
4) 108 ÷ 3 = ____
5) 558 ÷ 9 = ____

1) 60 2) 70 3) 45 4) 36 5) 62

Short multiplication

SATs example

5 9 × 41 =

1 mark

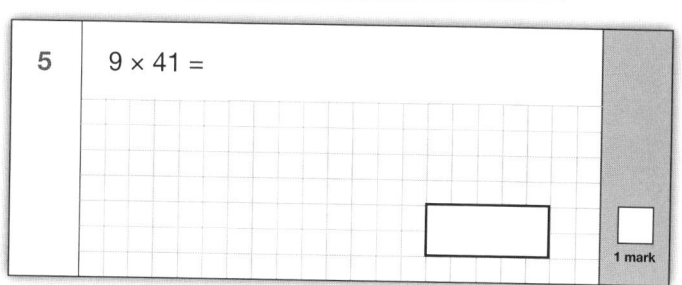

Explanation

Simple multiplication problems have a **multiplicand** (the larger number being multiplied) and the **multiplier** (the number we are multiplying by). The answer is the **product**. In 9 × 41, we are essentially working out the total of 9 groups of 41.

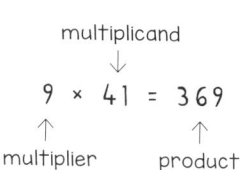

multiplicand
↓
9 × 41 = 369
↑   ↑
multiplier product

How to solve it

Short multiplication

Use short multiplication to solve the question.

For more detail on how to perform short multiplication, see page 46 of *Maths Like a Ninja*.

```
    4 1
×     9
─────
  3 6 9
```

Using related facts

You can use 'related facts' (your knowledge of your times tables) to answer using the partition and jot method. Partition means to separate; jot means to make notes. For example:

9 × 41

40 × 9 = ?   1 × 9 = ?

4 × 9 = 36

so 40 × 9 = 360

360 + 9 = 369

NINJA TIP:
Watch out for questions where the product is missing, but it is shown first in the question. Don't worry, just answer as normal. For example:
___ = 596 × 7.

Practice TASK

1) 34 × 5 = ___
2) 4 × 62 = ___
3) 7 × 83 = ___
4) 5 × 142 = ___
5) 3 × 326 = ___

1) 170 2) 248 3) 581, 4) 710 5) 978

MATHS

REASONING

Decimal addition

SATs example

6. 6.48 + 8.6 =

1 mark

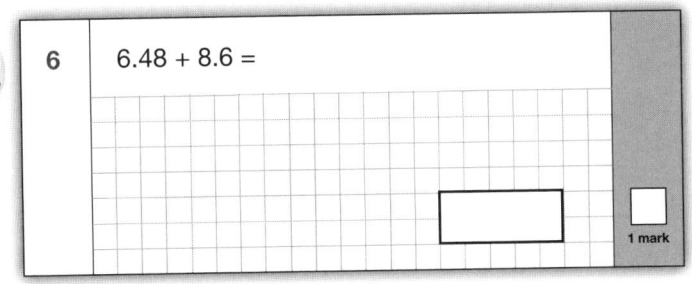

Explanation

Decimal addition is just the same process as normal column addition (see p. 86). The only difference is that you need to look closely at exactly how you lay out the numbers in the question.

NINJA TIP: Think about it like this: decimals live in their own house, on the same street.

How to solve it

Step 1: Write down three decimal spaces on top of each other in the middle of the working box. By doing this, we create an accurate place value chart and can place the numbers from the question correctly.

H	T	O	t	h

Step 2: In these questions, some numbers will likely have different amounts of digits and so there will be missing numbers. In these spaces, we use a place-holding zero.

H	T	O	t	h
		6	4	8
+		8	6	

Step 3: Carry out the addition or subtraction as normal.

H	T	O	t	h
		6	4	8
		8	6	0
	1	5	0	8
		1	1	

Practice TASK

1) 3.45 − 1.7 = ____
2) 9.341 − 4.98 = ____
3) 17.56 + 8.9 = ____
4) 5.914 + 1.03 = ____

1) 1.75 2) 4.361 3) 26.46 4) 6.944

Decimal subtraction from whole numbers

SATs example

19 | 7 − 2.25 =

1 mark

Explanation

Subtracting from whole numbers can seem tricky. The key thing is to first look at which digits are the ones. In the SATs example, 7 is a one, and 2 is a one.

$$(7) - (2).25 = ?$$

ones

How to solve it

H	T	O	t	h
−				

Step 1: Write down three decimal spaces on top of each other in the middle of the working box. By doing this, we create an accurate place value chart and can place the numbers from the question correctly.

H	T	O	t	h
		7	0	0
−		2	2	5

Step 2: In these questions, the whole number will leave missing numbers and so there will be some spaces. In these spaces, we use a place-holding zero.

H	T	O	t	h
		⁶7	¹9	¹0
−		2	2	5
		4	7	5

Step 3: Carry out the subtraction as normal.

SATs TIP
Remember to use your knowledge of subtraction and exchanging here.

Practice TASK

1) 7 − 1.45 = _____

2) 14 − 9.04 = _____

3) 8 − 1.726 = _____

4) 24 − 17.83 = _____

1) 5.55 2) 4.96 3) 6.274 4) 6.17

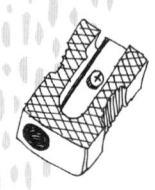

Multiplying and dividing by 10, 100 and 1,000

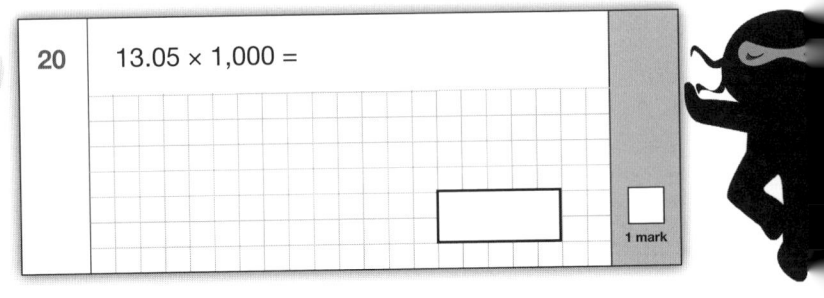

SATs example

20	13.05 × 1,000 =

1 mark

SATs example

16	2.12 ÷ 10 =

1 mark

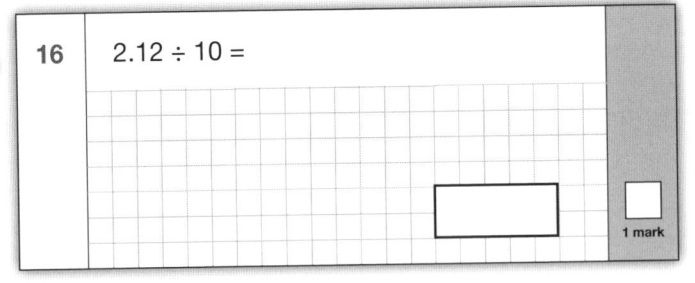

Explanation

Multiplying or dividing by 10, 100 or 1,000 is simply a test of your understanding of place value. With a little practice, these questions can be very straightforward to answer.

How to solve it

Each time a digit moves one column to the left, it becomes 10 times bigger (multiplication). Each time a digit moves one column to the right, it becomes 10 times smaller (division). If you move a digit two columns, it becomes 100 times bigger or smaller. If you move three times to the left or right, it becomes 1,000 times bigger or smaller. So, if you are multiplying by 1,000 you know you must move the digits three places to the left.

Step 1: Write two decimals on top of each other.

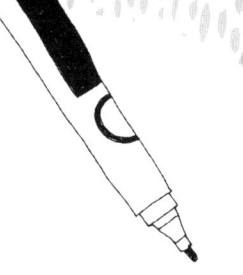

TTh	Th	H	T	O	.	t	h	th
					.			
					.			

Step 2: Write the number from the question.

TTh	Th	H	T	O	.	t	h	th
			1	3	.	0	5	
					.			

TTh	Th	H	T	O	.	t	h	th
				2	.	1	2	
					.			

Step 3: Move all the numbers one, two or three places to the left (multiplication) or right (division)

TTh	Th	H	T	O	.	t	h	th
			1	3	.	0	5	
1	3	0	5	0	.	0	0	

TTh	Th	H	T	O	.	t	h	th
				2	.	1	2	
				0	.	2	1	2

NINJA TIP:
Lots of pupils try to use short division (bus stop method) for these questions, but it won't work very well. You'll end up in a bit of a muddle and waste precious time.

SATS TIP
Look at 10, 100 and 1,000. The number of zeros in each of these numbers is telling you how many spaces to move right for division. 10 has one zero so you need to move all numbers one column. 100 has two zeros, so move all numbers two columns. 1,000 has three zeros, so move all numbers three columns right.

Practice TASK

1) 324 ÷ 10.0 = _____

2) 14.6 ÷ 10 = _____

3) 6.3 × 1,000 = _____

4) 0.56 × 100 = _____

5) 344 × 100 = _____

1) 32.4 2) 1.46 3) 6,300 4) 56 5) 34,400

Finding 10% and 5% (and multiples of 10)

SATs example

27 15% of 3,200 =

1 mark

Explanation

The most basic percentages questions will require you to find 10% of a number, or multiples of 10 such as 20% or 60%. They may also ask you to find 5%.

How to solve it

Finding 10%

You can find 10% of a number by using place value. To find 10%, you just need to divide the number by 10. This means that on a place value grid, each digit becomes 10 times smaller, so moves one column to the right. So, to find 10% of 3,000

Th	H	T	O	.	t	h
3	0	0	0	.	0	0
	3	0	0	.	0	0

Finding 20% or 60% (or any other multiple of 10)

To find 20%, find 10%, then multiply the number by 2. To find 60%, find 10% and then multiply the number by 6. So, to find 20% of 3,000:

10% of 3,000 = 300

300 × 2 = 600

So, 20% of 3,000 = 600

Finding 5%

This is easy. Find 10% and then halve the number.

You can combine the information you know to find trickier percentages. So, to find 65% of 120:

10% of 120 = 12; 12 × 6 = 72 (60%)

12 ÷ 2 = 6, therefore 5% of 120 = 6

72 + 6 = 78, therefore 65% of 120 = 78

Practice TASK

1) 10% of 45 = _____
2) 10% of 340 = _____
3) 20% of 240 = _____
4) 45% of 180 = _____
5) 85% of 260 = _____

1) 4.5 2) 34 3) 48 4) 81 5) 221

Finding 1%, 2%, 3% and 4%

SATs example

28 | 2% of 3,000 =

1 mark

Explanation

Finding 1% is a test of your ability to divide by 100. When you divide by 100, you will find 1% of a number.

How to solve it

Finding 1%
Using your knowledge of place value (p. 90), divide the number by 100.
So, to find 1% of 1,200:

Th	H	T	O	.	t	h
1	2	0	0	.		
		1	2	.	0	0

Finding 2%, 3% or 4%
Once you have found 1%, you can find 2% by just doubling your 1% value.

Find 4% by doubling your 2% value.

Find 3% by adding your 1% and 2% values together.

1% of 1,200 = 12
2 × 12 (1%) = 24 (2%)
12 (1%) + 24 (2%) = 36 (3%)
2 × 24 (2%) = 48 (4%)

Practice TASK

1) 1% of 2,400 = ____
2) 1% of 360 = ____
3) 2% of 2,800 = ____
4) 3% of 4,500 = ____
5) 4% of 760 = ____

1) 24 2) 3.6 3) 56 4) 135 5) 30.4

Finding complex percentages

SATs example 34 28% of 650 =

1 mark

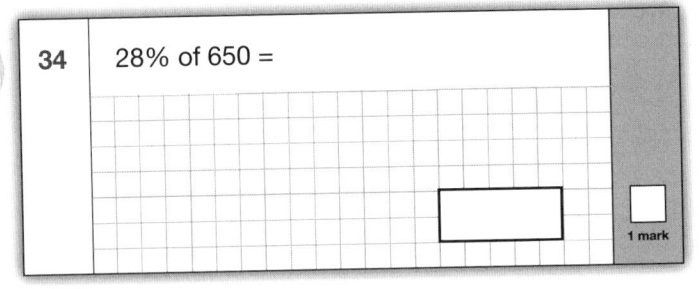

Explanation

Remember the percentages you can easily find, such as 10%, 5%, 1% and 2%. You can use these to find any other percentage by multiplying and adding.

> **SATS TIP**
> Complex percentages can involve many steps and opportunities to make mistakes as you try to find 10%, 1%, 5%, 3%, 8% and 20% to find the answer.

How to solve it

Instead of muliplying and adding, you can try this two-step strategy using long multiplication and dividing the answer by 100. So, to find 28% of 650:

Step 1: Multiply the numbers together using long multiplication (see p. 117).

```
        6 5 0
    ×     2 8
    ---------
      5 ⁴2 0 0
    1 ¹3 0 0 0
    ---------
    1 8 2 0 0
```

Step 2: Use your knowledge of place value (p. 90) to divide the number by 100.

TTh	Th	H	T	O	.	t	h	th
1	8	2	0	0	.			
		1	8	2	.	0	0	

So, the answer to 28% of 650 is 182.

Practice TASK

1) 26% of 450 = ____
2) 37% of 190 = ____
3) 67% of 270 = ____
4) 44% of 440 = ____
5) 83% of 250 = ____

1) 117 2) 70.3 3) 180.9 4) 193.6 5) 207.5

Multiplying and dividing by 0 and 1

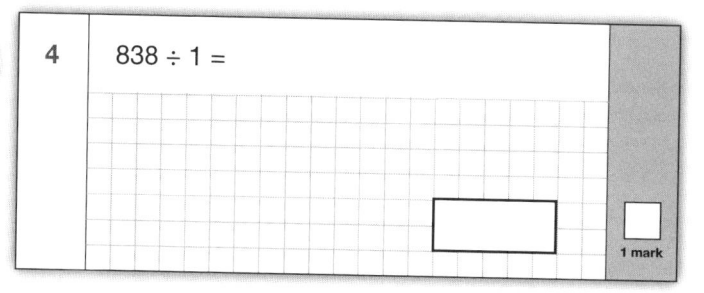

SATs example

9   213 × 0 =

1 mark

SATs example

4   838 ÷ 1 =

1 mark

Explanation

Multiplying and dividing by 1 and 0 are simple concepts to master; you just need to concentrate and these questions will be extremely simple and easy marks.

How to solve it

Dividing and multiplying by 0
When we multiply or divide by zero, the answer is always zero. These questions always come up in arithmetic tests, so be sure to focus and take the easy marks.

452 × 0 = 0; 13 × 0 = 0; 1,926 ÷ 0 = 0

Dividing or multiplying by 1
When we multiply or divide a number by 1, the answer will always be the same as the number in the question.

671 × 1 = 671; 14 ÷ 1 = 14; 1,761 × 1 = 1,761

Practice TASK

1) 1,431 ÷ 0 = _____
2) 421 ÷ 0 = _____
3) 46 × 1 = _____
4) 6,031 × 1 = _____

1) 0 2) 0 3) 46 4) 6,031

Square and cube numbers

SATs example

16 | $3^3 =$

	1 mark

Explanation

A square number is a number that has been multiplied by itself. For example, $2^2 = 2 \times 2 = 4$

A cube number is a number that has been multiplied by itself and then by itself again. For example, $2^3 = 2 \times 2 \times 2 = 8$

How to solve it

Square numbers are essentially number facts. So, the aim is to just try to learn these.

$1^2 = 1 \times 1 = 1$
$2^2 = 2 \times 2 = 4$
$3^2 = 3 \times 3 = 9$
$4^2 = 4 \times 4 = 16$
$5^2 = 5 \times 5 = 25$
$6^2 = 6 \times 6 = 36$
$7^2 = 7 \times 7 = 49$
$8^2 = 8 \times 8 = 64$
$9^2 = 9 \times 9 = 81$
$10^2 = 10 \times 10 = 100$
$11^2 = 11 \times 11 = 121$
$12^2 = 12 \times 12 = 144$

Cube numbers, just like square numbers, never change so you can just learn them.

$1^3 = 1 \times 1 \times 1 = 1$
$2^3 = 2 \times 2 \times 2 = 8$
$3^3 = 3 \times 3 \times 3 = 27$
$4^3 = 4 \times 4 \times 4 = 64$
$5^3 = 5 \times 5 \times 5 = 125$
$6^3 = 6 \times 6 \times 6 = 216$
$7^3 = 7 \times 7 \times 7 = 343$
$8^3 = 8 \times 8 \times 8 = 512$
$9^3 = 9 \times 9 \times 9 = 729$
$10^3 = 10 \times 10 \times 10 = 1,000$
$11^3 = 11 \times 11 \times 11 = 1,331$
$12^3 = 12 \times 12 \times 12 = 1,728$

SATS TIP

The square ^{2} doesn't mean 'times 2'; it means 'multiplied by itself'. So 7^2 means 7×7 (which is 49), not 7×2 (which is 14).

Multiplying fractions

SATs example

16    $\frac{4}{6} \times \frac{3}{5} =$

1 mark

Explanation

Multiplying fractions together is so much easier than you might expect. You'll be a fractions master before you know it.

Remember, the number on the top of a fraction is called the numerator and the number on the bottom of a fraction is called the denominator.

How to solve it

When you have a question that wants you to multiply two fractions together, all you need to do is multiply the numerators from both fractions together to create a new numerator. Then multiply both denominators together to get a new denominator.

$4 \times 3 = 12$

$\frac{4}{6} \times \frac{3}{5} = \frac{12}{30}$

$6 \times 5 = 30$

NINJA TIP: Sometimes you can simplify the fraction answer using a common factor.

$2 \times 1 = 2$

$\frac{2}{5} \times \frac{1}{3} = \frac{2}{15}$

$5 \times 3 = 15$

Practice TASK

1) $\frac{4}{5} \times \frac{1}{4} =$ _____

2) $\frac{3}{6} \times \frac{4}{5} =$ _____

3) $\frac{9}{10} \times \frac{3}{6} =$ _____

4) $\frac{4}{8} \times \frac{6}{11} =$ _____

1) $\frac{4}{20}$ 2) $\frac{12}{30}$ 3) $\frac{27}{60}$ 4) $\frac{24}{88}$

Dividing fractions by whole numbers

SATs example

24) $\frac{1}{8} \div 2 =$

1 mark

Explanation

Dividing fractions by whole numbers is another problem that can look quite scary, but in fact, it's one of the simplest maths problems to answer.

It is important to remember what is happening when you divide: when you divide, the number or fraction you are working with becomes smaller. So, you have LESS. Would you rather have $\frac{1}{2}$ of £100 or $\frac{1}{10}$ of £100? Well, $\frac{1}{2}$ obviously! But notice that as the denominator gets larger, the amount we are working with gets smaller. Remember, the denominator shows us the equal parts of the whole.

How to solve it

To solve this problem, simply multiply the denominator (bottom number) by the whole number. With multiplying and dividing fractions by whole numbers, we always multiply. Even though the symbol in the question is divide.

$\frac{1}{8} \div 2 = \frac{1}{16}$
x together

$\frac{4}{5} \div 3 = \frac{4}{15}$
x together

NINJA TIP:
Remember, the number on the top of a fraction is called the numerator and the number on the bottom is called the denominator.

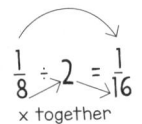

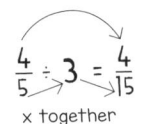

SATs TIP
Not sure which number to multiply? Divide begins with 'd' and so does denominator! So if it's a **d**ivide, you need to multiply the **d**enominator.

Practice TASK

1) $\frac{1}{3} \div 4 =$ ___   2) $\frac{3}{4} \div 5 =$ ___

3) $\frac{2}{7} \div 6 =$ ___

1) $\frac{1}{12}$ 2) $\frac{3}{20}$ 3) $\frac{2}{42}$

104

Multiplying fractions by whole numbers

SATs example

36. $\frac{4}{5} \times 6 =$

1 mark

Explanation

It is important to remember what is happening when you multiply. The number or fraction you are working with becomes greater. So, you have MORE.

The numerator represents how much of the fraction you have. So, you should expect this to become greater.

How to solve it

To solve this problem, simply multiply the numerator (top number) by the whole number.

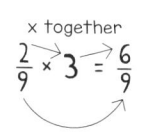

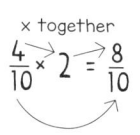

× together: $\frac{2}{9} \times 3 = \frac{6}{9}$

× together: $\frac{4}{10} \times 2 = \frac{8}{10}$

With this type of question, you may create an answer that is an improper fraction, where the numerator (top number) is larger than the denominator (bottom number). You must convert an improper fraction to a mixed number by dividing the denominator (bottom number) into the larger numerator (top number). For example:

$\frac{7}{5} = \frac{5}{5}$ or 1

$\frac{2}{5} = 1\frac{2}{5}$

Practice TASK

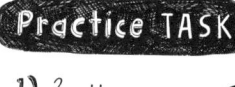

1) $\frac{2}{9} \times 4 =$ ____

2) $\frac{1}{7} \times 5 =$ ____

3) $\frac{2}{10} \times 3 =$ ____

1) $\frac{8}{9}$ 2) $\frac{5}{7}$ 3) $\frac{6}{10}$

SATS TIP
Not sure which number to multiply? If it's a times (×) question, times begins with 't' and so does top. So multiply the top number! Yup, the numerator.

Finding fractions of amounts

SATs example

22 $\frac{7}{10} \times 30 =$

1 mark

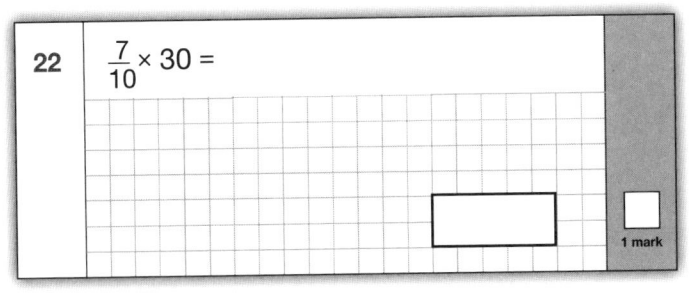

Explanation

Finding fractions of amounts might seem tricky, but as long as you know your times tables, it can be straightforward.

How to solve it

Written strategy

All you need to do is divide the number involved by the denominator (bottom number) and multiply the answer by the numerator (top number). For example:

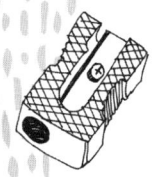

$\frac{7}{10}$ of 30

Step 1: divide 30 by 10 = 3

Step 2: multiply 3 by 7 = 21

So, $\frac{7}{10}$ of 30 is 21

Mental strategy (using known facts)

You can use 'known facts' (your knowledge of your times tables and place number) to answer these questions. For example:

$\frac{4}{6}$ of 2,400 might seem tricky. But if you work with 24 rather than 2,400 (making the number 100 times smaller), you can more easily work out the answer.

$\frac{4}{6}$ of 2,400 ← this seems tricky!

Step 1: 24 ÷ 6 = 4 (24 is 100 times smaller than 2,400)

Step 2: 4 (numerator) × 4 = 16

So, $\frac{4}{6}$ of 24 = 16

Step 3: Now make it 100 times bigger again:
16 × 100 = 1,600

So, $\frac{4}{6}$ of 2,400 = 1,600

SATS TIP
Often, you can calculate these mentally by just working with known times tables facts.

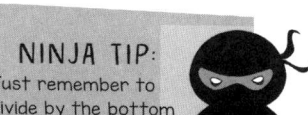

NINJA TIP:
Just remember to divide by the bottom and times by the top! That's it!

Practice TASK

1) $\frac{3}{5}$ of 150 = ____

2) $\frac{2}{7}$ of 28 = ____

1) 90   2) 8

Adding and subtracting fractions with the same denominator

SATs example

2) $\frac{9}{11} + \frac{4}{11} =$

1 mark

Explanation

Questions that ask you to add or subtract fractions with the same denominator offer easy marks in SATs. If the denominators (the bottom numbers) are the same, you can just go ahead and add or subtract the numerators (the top numbers) together.

How to solve it

Add or subtract the numerators. The denominator stays the same. Simple!

$$\frac{4}{9} + \frac{3}{9} = \frac{7}{9} \qquad \frac{6}{11} + \frac{2}{11} = \frac{8}{11} \qquad \frac{8}{11} - \frac{2}{11} = \frac{6}{11} \qquad \frac{14}{15} - \frac{9}{15} = \frac{5}{15}$$

Sometimes when you add fractions, you can end up with a numerator that is larger than the denominator. This is called an improper fraction. To ensure you get all the marks available, you need to convert this improper fraction into a mixed number. To do this, divide the denominator into the numerator. For example:

$$\frac{7}{9} + \frac{4}{9} = \frac{11}{9}$$

How many 9s are in 11? 1 whole, with 2 parts left over. So, this is 1 and $\frac{2}{9}$.

$\frac{9}{9}$ or 1 $\frac{2}{9}$ $\boxed{11} = 1\frac{2}{9}$

Practice TASK

1) $\frac{2}{7} + \frac{3}{7} =$ ____   2) $\frac{12}{13} - \frac{7}{13} =$ ____

3) $\frac{5}{9} + \frac{7}{9} =$ ____   4) $\frac{9}{10} + \frac{2}{10} =$ ____

1) $\frac{5}{7}$ 2) $\frac{5}{13}$ 3) $1\frac{3}{9}$ 4) $1\frac{1}{10}$

NINJA TIP: If the denominators are the same, we're in the game!

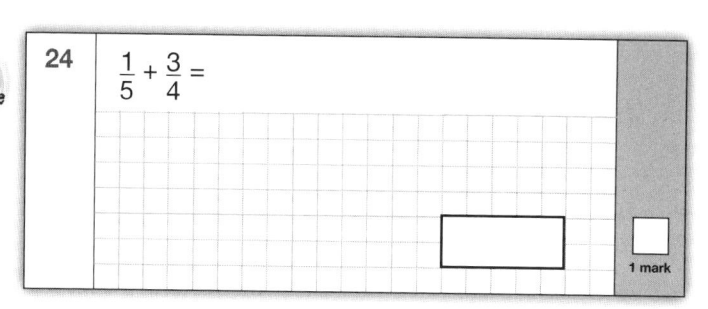

Adding and subtracting fractions with different denominators

SATs example 24 $\dfrac{1}{5} + \dfrac{3}{4} =$

1 mark

SATs example 31 $\dfrac{2}{7} - \dfrac{1}{9} =$

1 mark

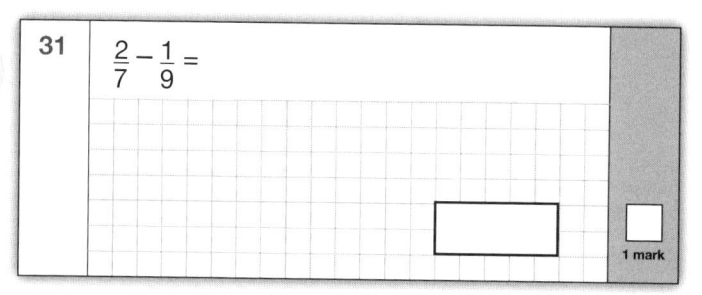

Explanation

The first thing to do with fraction questions is to look at the denominators. If they are the same, simply add or subtract the numerator (see p. 108). If the denominators are different, you'll need to do a bit more work.

How to solve it

Step 1: Find a common denominator (the lowest common multiple). You can do this by writing out each denominator's times table until you find a multiple that they share.

$$\dfrac{1}{5} + \dfrac{3}{4}$$

Times table for 5: 5, 10, 15, **20**
Times table for 4: 4, 8, 12, 16, **20**

Step 2: Rewrite the question with the new denominators. Leave the numerator blank. Draw an arrow from the original denominator to the new denominator. Work out what you need to multiply the original denominator by to get to the new one (just think of your times tables).

$$\times 4 \left(\frac{1}{5} + \frac{3}{4} \right) \times 5$$
$$ \frac{}{20} + \frac{}{20}$$

Step 3: Once you know what you need to multiply the old denominator by, multiply the numerators by the same numbers to get your new numerators.

$$\times 4 \left(\frac{1}{5} + \frac{3}{4} \right) \times 5$$
$$ \frac{4}{20} + \frac{15}{20}$$

Step 4: Don't forget to solve the original question! In this case:

$$\frac{1}{5} + \frac{3}{4} = \frac{4}{20} + \frac{15}{20} = \frac{19}{20}$$

NINJA TIP:
You are basically multiplying the denominator and numerator by the same number. A good way to remember it is this: 'whatever you do to the bottom, do to the top'.

Adding fractions and mixed numbers

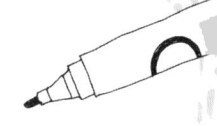

SATs example

21 $\frac{2}{3} + 2\frac{1}{3} =$

1 mark

Explanation

The first thing to look for is the denominators. If they are the same, it's much easier.

How to solve it

Same denominator
Convert the mixed number into an improper fraction by multiplying the whole number by the denominator. Add your answer to the existing numerator. For example:

$$\frac{2}{3} + 2\frac{1}{3}$$

$2\frac{1}{3}$ 2 (whole number) × 3 (denominator) = 6
6 + 1 (numerator) = 7

So, $2\frac{1}{3} = \frac{7}{3}$

Now answer the original question: $\frac{2}{3} + \frac{7}{3} = \frac{9}{3} = 3$

Since $\frac{9}{3}$ is an improper fraction, you need to simplify it. How many 3s in 9? 3.

Different denominator
If the fraction and the mixed number have different denominators, you need to convert the mixed number into an improper fraction and find a common denominator. Then, simply follow the steps for adding fractions with different denominators (see p. 109).

Subtracting fractions from mixed numbers

SATs example

22. $1\frac{3}{7} - \frac{4}{7} =$

1 mark

Explanation
The first thing to look at is the denominators. If they are the same, it's much easier.

How to solve it

Same denominator
Convert the mixed number into an improper fraction by multiplying the whole number by the denominator. Add your answer to the existing numerator. For example:

$$1\frac{3}{7} - \frac{4}{7}$$

$1\frac{3}{7}$ 1 (whole number) x 7 (denominator) = 7   7 + 3 (numerator) = 10

So, $1\frac{3}{7} = \frac{10}{7}$

Now answer the original question: $\frac{10}{7} - \frac{4}{7} = \frac{6}{7}$

Different denominator
If the fraction and the mixed number have different denominators, you need to convert the mixed number into an improper fraction and find a common denominator. Then, simply follow the steps for subtracting fractions with different denominators (see p. 109).

Adding and subtracting mixed numbers

Method 1

Convert to an improper fraction

NINJA TIP: To do this, find a common denominator.

Step 1: Convert both mixed numbers to improper fractions.

Example: $2\frac{1}{3} + 1\frac{1}{2} = ?$

→ See page 111 for this.

$2\frac{1}{3} = \frac{7}{3}$ $\qquad$ $1\frac{1}{2} = \frac{3}{2}$

Step 2: Find the lowest common denominator of the two improper fractions. It's 6.

$3 \times 2 = 6$
$2 \times 3 = 6$

Step 3: Multiply the numerator of each fraction by the same amount as the denominator has been multiplied.

$\frac{7}{3} \xrightarrow{\times 2} \frac{14}{6}$ $\qquad$ $\frac{3}{2} \xrightarrow{\times 3} \frac{9}{6}$

Step 4: Add the fractions together. $\qquad \frac{14}{6} + \frac{9}{6} = \frac{23}{6}$

Step 5: Convert back to a mixed number. $\qquad \frac{23}{6} = 3\frac{5}{6}$

NINJA TIP:
This works in exactly the same way for subtraction too.

Adding and subtracting mixed numbers

Method 2

Partition the mixed numbers

Step 1: Partition (separate) the whole numbers from the fractions.

Example: $2\frac{1}{3} + 1\frac{1}{2} = ?$

$2\frac{1}{3} = 2 + \frac{1}{3}$ $1\frac{1}{2} = 1 + \frac{1}{2}$

NINJA TIP: This works in the same way for subtraction.

Step 2: Add the whole numbers. $2 + 1 = 3$

Step 3: Find the lowest common denominator of the two proper fractions. It's 6.

$3 \times 2 = 6$
$2 \times 3 = 6$

Step 4: Multiply the numerator of each fraction by the same amount as the denominator has been multiplied.

$\frac{1}{3} \xrightarrow{\times 2} \frac{2}{6}$ $\frac{1}{2} \xrightarrow{\times 3} \frac{3}{6}$

Step 5: Add the fractions together. $\frac{2}{6} + \frac{3}{6} = \frac{5}{6}$

Step 6: Don't forget to add the whole number total from Step 2 to the final mixed number.

$3 + \frac{5}{6} = 3\frac{5}{6}$ $2\frac{1}{3} + 1\frac{1}{2} = 3\frac{5}{6}$

Multiplying mixed numbers

SATs example

34   $1\frac{3}{4} \times 10 =$

1 mark

Explanation

Multiplying mixed numbers is pretty straightforward. Just remember how to multiply fractions by whole numbers (see p. 105) and you are pretty much there!

How to solve it

Partition method

The most simple way to solve these questions is to partition the mixed number into a whole number and a fraction, and multiply them separately. Then add the two parts together again to answer the problem. Here's an example.

$1\frac{3}{4} \times 10 = ?$

$1\frac{3}{4} = 1 + \frac{3}{4}$

$1 \times 10 = 10$ $\frac{3}{4} \times 10 = \frac{30}{4} = 7\frac{2}{4}$

$10 + 7\frac{2}{4} = 17\frac{2}{4}$

Convert to an improper fraction

$1\frac{3}{4} \times 10 = ?$

$4 \times 1 + 3 = 7$

$1\frac{3}{4} = \frac{7}{4}$

$\frac{7}{4} \times 10 = \frac{70}{4}$

How many 4s in 70? (Use short division, p. 91.)

$\frac{70}{4} = 17\frac{2}{4}$

SATS TIP

Remember, when you multiply fractions by whole numbers, you multiply the numerator!

BODMAS

SATs example

15) $60 \div (30 - 24) =$

[1 mark]

Explanation

BODMAS and BIDMAS are acronyms to help us remember the correct order to carry out calculation operations, such as add or subtract. You need to be aware of BODMAS when answering questions that contain different operations.

B	O	D	M	A	S
Brackets	Order	Divide	Multiply	Add	Subtract
( )	$\sqrt{x}$ or x^2	÷	×	+	−

B	I	D	M	A	S
Brackets	Indices	Divide	Multiply	Add	Subtract
( )	$\sqrt{x}$ or x^2	÷	×	+	−

Try rewriting calculations until you only have two numbers and one operation remaining.

$2^2 + 4 \times 3 = ?$
$4 + 4 \times 3 = ?$
$4 + 12 = 16$

Practice TASK

1) $6 + 4 \div 2 = $ ____
2) $3^2 \times 12 - 5 = $ ____
3) $15 - 3 \times 4 = $ ____

1) 8 2) 103 3) 3

NINJA TIP:
BODMAS and BIDMAS are the same thing. The 'O' in BODMAS refers to 'order' and the 'I' in BIDMAS refers to 'indices'.

Long multiplication

SATs example

33   4 0 7 8
       ×   6 7

Show your method

2 marks

Explanation

Note the crucial comment on the left-hand side of the working space. You must show your method to get all the available points for this question.

How to solve it

Step 1: Write out the question with the biggest number on top. Example: 24 × 35 = ?

```
      3 5
  ×   2 4
  ─────────
```

Step 2: Multiply the top digits by the ones digit on the bottom row. Start with the top ones column × bottom ones column. Then repeat for the top tens, top hundreds and so on.

```
      3 5
  ×   2 4
  ─────────
    1 ²4 0   (5 × 4 = 20, 30 × 4 = 120)
```

Step 3: Write 0 in the ones column of the second answer row before you start. Multiply the numbers on the top row by the tens on the bottom row. Start with the top ones column × bottom tens column.

```
      3 5
  ×   2 4
  ─────────
    1 ²4 0   (5 × 4 = 20, 30 × 4 = 120)
  + ¹7 0 ⓪   (5 × 20 = 100, 30 × 20 = 600)
```

↑ This place-holding zero will help you keep the place value accurate.

Step 4: Add up both answer rows using column addition.

```
      3 5
  ×   2 4
  ─────────
    1 ²4 0
  + ¹7 0 0
  ─────────
    8 4 0
```

Long division

SATs example

17 2 1) 6 7 2

Show your method

2 marks

Explanation

If you don't know the times table for the divisor number that you need to work with (in this case 21), then you can use partial tables to help you.

Note the crucial comment on the left-hand side of the working space. You must show your method to get all the available points for this question.

How to solve it

Step 1: Create a partial table for the divisor, and fill it in, to support you in the next step.

×	21
1	21
2	42	) × 2
4	84	) × 2
10	210	) ÷ 2
5	105

Step 2: Subtract multiples of the divisor from the dividend. In brackets, write how many lots of the divisor are in the chunk. Repeat until you can no longer subtract the divisor.

```
21 ) 6 7 2
     2 1 0   (10 × 21)
     4 6 2
     4 2 0   (20 × 21)
     0 4 2
       4 2   (2 × 21)
         0
```

Step 3: Add up how many lots of the divisor you used from your notes in brackets. This is the answer. Anything left over is a remainder (r). In this case, the answer is 32.

Long division

SATs example

29

7 3) 3 0 6 6

Show your method

2 marks

Explanation

If you don't know the times table for the divisor number you need to work with (in this case 73), then you can use partial tables to help you.

Note the crucial comment on the left-hand side of the working space. You must show your method to get all the available points for this question.

How to solve it

Step 1: Create a partial table for the divisor, and fill it in, to support you in the next step.

×	73
1	73
2	146
4	292
10	730
5	365

) × 2
) × 2
) ÷ 2

Step 2: Subtract multiples of the divisor from the dividend. In brackets, write how many lots of the divisor are in the chunk. Repeat until you can no longer subtract the divisor.

```
73)3 0 6 6
     7 3 0   (10 × 73)
   2 3 3 6
   2 1 9 0   (30 × 73)
     1 4 6
     1 4 6   (2 × 73)
           0
```

Step 3: Add up how many lots of the divisor you used from your notes in brackets. This is the answer. Anything left over is a remainder (r). In this case, the answer is 42.

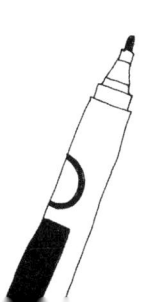

Reasoning

Mathematics: Papers 2 and 3 reasoning

Test details

Test day - Wednesday (after the arithmetic paper) and Thursday

Time allowed - 40 minutes on Wednesday and 40 on minutes on Thursday

Number of questions - Questions have varied between 21 and 25 questions. Questions can be worth one, two or three marks. Wednesday's paper is worth 35 marks and Thursday's paper is also worth 35 marks. 70 marks total.

The marks for this paper are combined with the marks for the arithmetic paper to give a combined mathematics mark out of 110.

Layout and appearance

The reasoning papers looks like this. You will find multiple questions on each page.

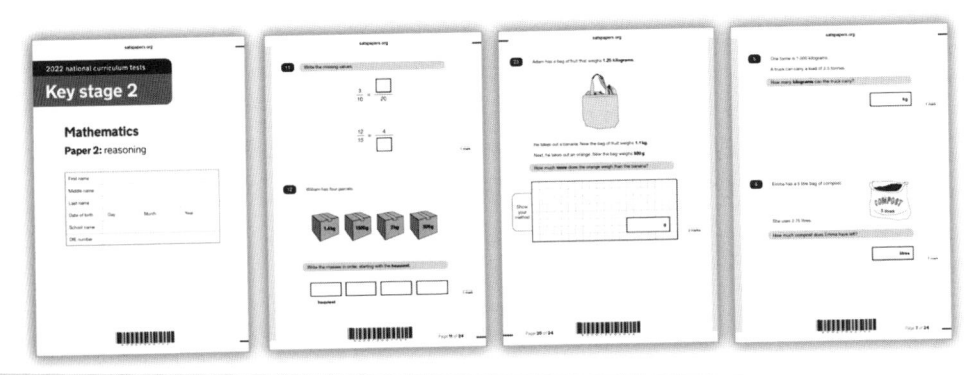

Example questions

The reasoning paper presents questions with written sentences and information presented in different ways, using images, graphs, shapes, tables and much more.

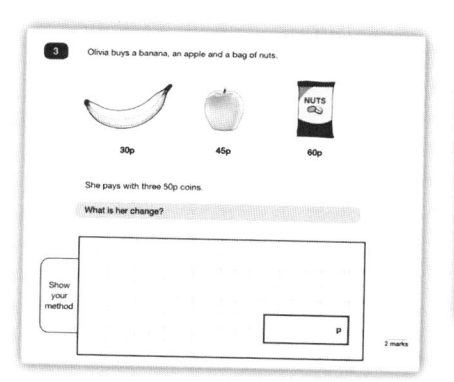

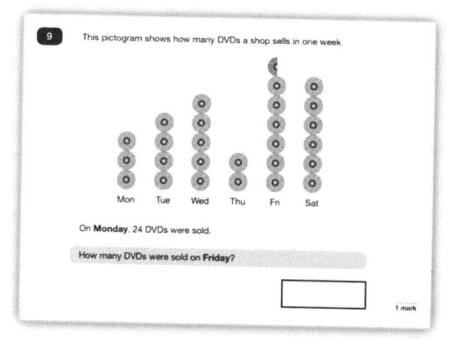

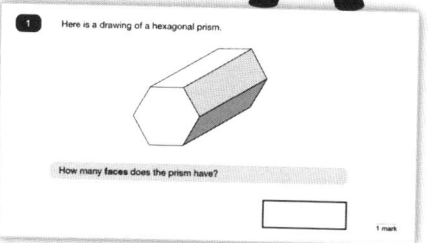

3 Olivia buys a banana, an apple and a bag of nuts.

| 30p | 45p | 60p |

She pays with three 50p coins.

What is her change?

Show your method

☐ p

2 marks

1 Here is a drawing of a hexagonal prism.

How many **faces** does the prism have?

☐

1 mark

9 This pictogram shows how many DVDs a shop sells in one week.

Mon Tue Wed Thu Fri Sat

On **Monday**, 24 DVDs were sold.

How many DVDs were sold on **Friday**?

☐

1 mark

4 Children estimated the number of beans in a jar.

These were the estimates of five children.

Amir	1,310
Olivia	1,220
Emma	1,400
John	1,290
Chen	1,460

The exact number of beans in the jar was **1,380**.

Whose estimate was **closest** to the exact number?

_____

1 mark

NINJA TIP:
It's important to put your answer in the answer box. If you don't, you won't get the mark, even if you have the correct answer.

SATS TIP
If a reasoning question is two or three marks, it means there will be two or three steps you need to take to answer the problem. This normally means you might need to carry out two or three different calculations to get to the answer.

REASONING

121

Number: Doubling and halving

Doubling and halving is a very important skill in SATs. Let's have a go at some:

Doubling

Some numbers are easier to double than others. For more complex numbers, try doubling the hundreds, tens and ones separately and then just adding them together again.

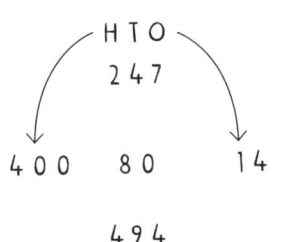

H T O
2 4 7
↓ ↓ ↓
4 0 0   8 0   1 4

4 9 4

NINJA TIP:
When the number is odd, it can be tricky to double. Try doubling the tens and ones separately. Use your times tables knowledge to help, just × 2.

Halving

When halving, if you can't halve a number in your head, use the same strategy as when you double a complex number. Make jottings and halve each place value separately.

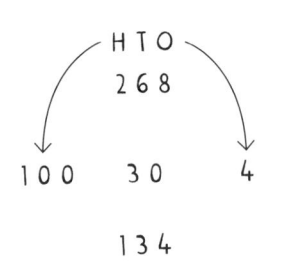

H T O
2 6 8
↓ ↓ ↓
1 0 0   3 0   4

1 3 4

NINJA TIP:
If you are halving an odd number, you will always end up with .5 as part of your answer.

SATS TIP
Make little notes on the paper as you double or halve the number, so you don't have to hold lots of facts in your head.

Practice TASK

1) Double 140 = ____
2) Double 167 = ____
3) Halve 260 = ____
4) Halve 593 = ____

1) 280 2) 334 3) 130 4) 296.5

Number: Multiples and related facts

Before your **SATs** tests, you should know all your times tables facts confidently. The reasoning paper often has questions that link directly to your knowledge of times tables facts and your understanding of multiples and related facts.

For example, if you know that 6 x 7 = 42, you should be able to use this to help you solve 6 x 70 or 60 x 70, etc.

Questions involving this skill are very common.

Practice TASK

1) 450 ÷ 5 = ____
2) 90 x 50 = ____
3) 5 x 900 = ____
4) 450 ÷ 5 = ____

1) 90 2) 4,500 3) 4,500 4) 90

NINJA TIP:
It's a real skill to be able to spot times tables facts hidden in lots of SATs questions. If you can spot them, it will really help you solve reasoning problems.

Shape: 2D

It's important to know all of the shape facts below, as these will help you answer reasoning questions that involve shapes.

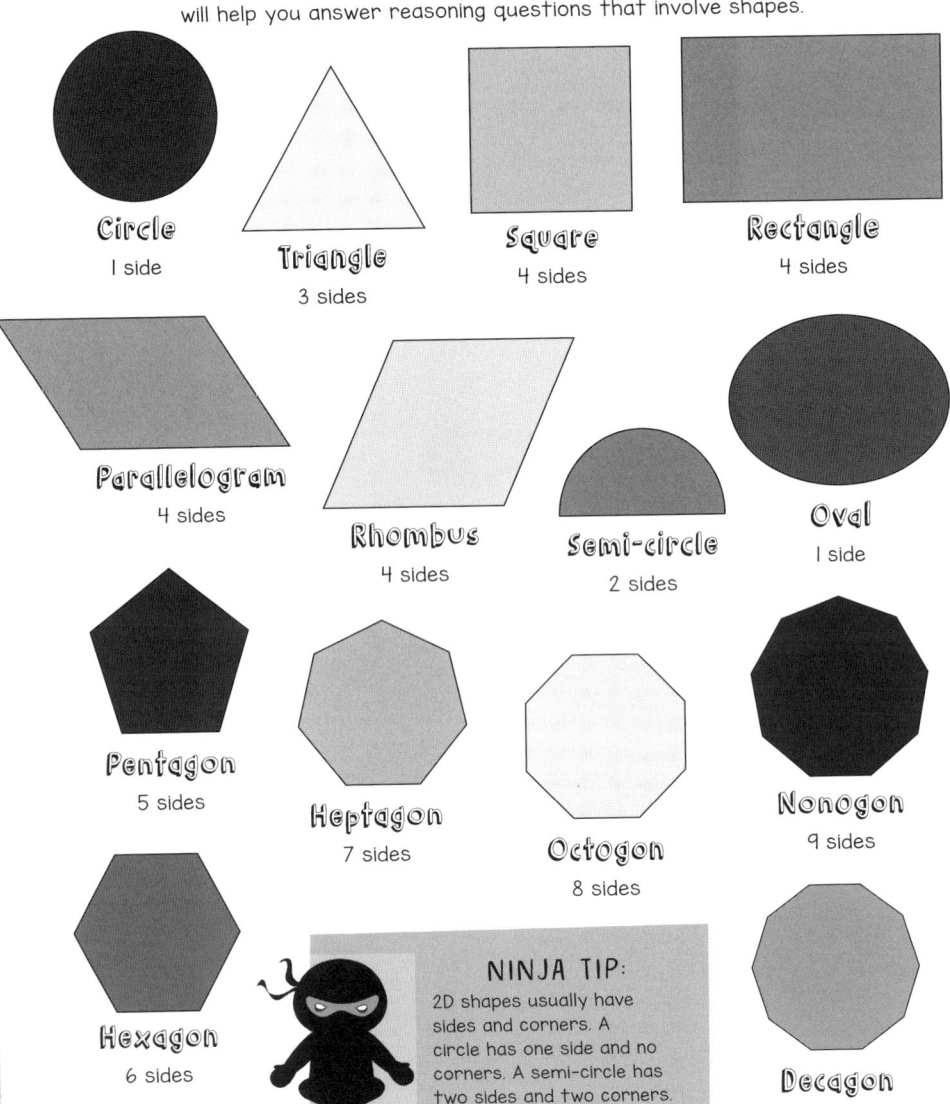

Circle — 1 side

Triangle — 3 sides

Square — 4 sides

Rectangle — 4 sides

Parallelogram — 4 sides

Rhombus — 4 sides

Semi-circle — 2 sides

Oval — 1 side

Pentagon — 5 sides

Heptagon — 7 sides

Octogon — 8 sides

Nonogon — 9 sides

Hexagon — 6 sides

Decagon — 10 sides

NINJA TIP:
2D shapes usually have sides and corners. A circle has one side and no corners. A semi-circle has two sides and two corners.

Shape: 3D

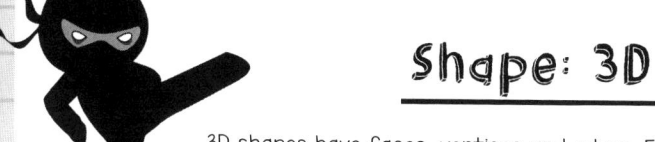

3D shapes have faces, vertices and edges. Faces are flat surfaces. Edges are the sides that define the shape and where faces meet. Vertices (corners) occur where edges meet.

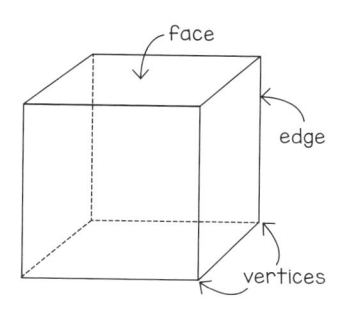

NINJA TIP: A sphere has no edges and one curved face.

	Tetrahedron	Cuboid	Triangular prism
Image			
Vertices	4	8	6
Edges	6	12	9
Faces	4	6	5

Measure and volume

Learning all of the measure facts on this page will help you answer reasoning questions that involve measure.

1 metre (m) = 100 centimetres (cm)

100 cm = 1 m

1 cm = 10 millimetres (mm)

10 mm = 1 cm

1 kilometre (km) = 1,000 m

1,000 m = 1 km

1,000 ml = 1 litre (L)

1 litre (L) = 1,000 ml

Half a litre = 500 ml

500 ml = Half a litre

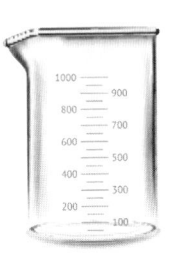

1,000 gram (g) = 1 kilogram (kg)

1 kg = 1,000 g

Half a kilogram (kg) = 500 g

500 g = Half a kilogram (kg)

1 mile = 1.6 kilometres (to convert miles to kilometres, just muliply by 1.6)

1 kilometre = 0.62 miles (to convert kilometres to miles, just divide by 1.6)

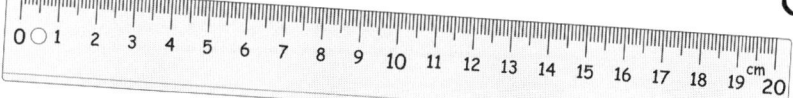

SATS TIP
SATs questions often require you to convert between measures, so you may need to covert from ml to L, or from g to kg to reach your answer.

NINJA TIP:
You can use your knowledge of place value and multiplication and divison to help you convert from one measure to another. For example, to convert grams to kilograms, you need to divide by 1,000.

SATs example

10 Jack fills a glass with 275 ml of water. Jill fills a bucket with 1.85 L of water. How many ml of water do Jack and Jill have in the containers altogether?

How to solve it

To solve this problem, you need to know there are 1000 ml in a L, and that 1 L is equal to 1000 ml. As the numbers in the question have different measures, you will need to convert one of them. Only then will you be able to add them together.

So, 1.85 L converts to 1,850 ml

1,850 ml + 275 ml = 2,125 ml

The answer is 2,125 ml.

Time

In a reasoning question about time, the question won't ask you how many minutes are in an hour, but it may be related to minutes and hours. Your knowledge of the 6 times table will help you answer questions about time.

Here are some basic time facts for you to learn.

Time

1 hour = 60 minutes

Half an hour = 30 minutes

Quarter of an hour = 15 minutes

1 minute = 60 seconds

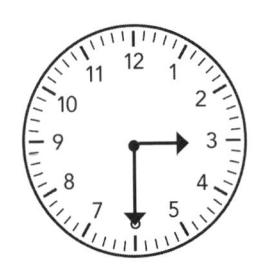

NINJA TIP:
To convert between the 12-hour and the 24-hour clock, just add or subtract 12 from the hours. So, a 24-hour clock showing 13:13 means 1.13 pm (you need to take 12 from 13).

SATS TIP
Practise converting seconds into hours using your knowledge of the 6 times table. For example, 246 seconds is 4 minutes and 6 seconds. Practise converting hours to minutes. For example, 2 hours and 36 minutes is 156 minutes.

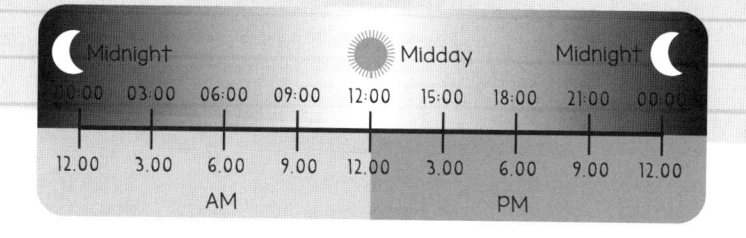

Years, months and weeks

7 days = 1 week

2 weeks = 1 fortnight

365 days = 1 year

52 weeks = 1 year

12 months = 1 year

Years and beyond

10 years = 1 decade

100 years = 1 century

1,000 years = 1 millennium

There are 12 months in a year:

January
February
March
April
May
June
July
August
September
October
November
December

SATs example

12 John rides his bicycle for 240 minutes. How many hours does John ride his bicycle for?

How to solve it

The question isn't telling you how to solve the problem. You need to use your knowledge of 60 minutes in an hour to solve the problem.

Using known facts, you might spot that 24 is in the 6 times table. 4 × 6 is 24, so 4 × 60 is 240. Alternatively, you could work out how many 60s are in 240. Either way, the answer is 4 hours.

Angles

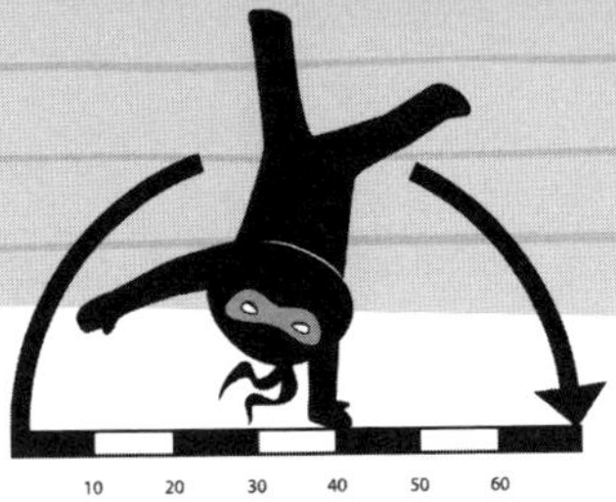

Angles occur where two lines meet or intersect. These angles can be measured using a protractor.

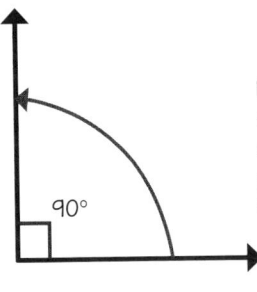

Right angles are angles that, when measured using a protractor, are **exactly 90°**.

90°

NINJA TIP:
Using a protractor can sometimes be tricky. Rotating the paper that the angle is printed on can help make it easier to measure.

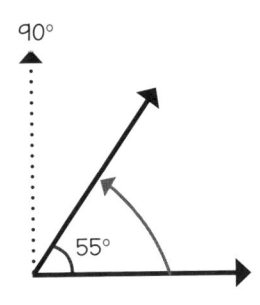

90°

Acute angles are angles that, when measured using a protractor, are **less than 90°**.

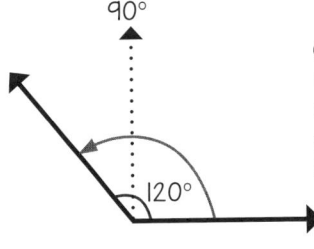

55°

90°

Obtuse angles are angles that, when measured using a protractor, are **between 90° and 180°**.

120°

SATS TIP
If the image of the shape or angle is small, extend the lines using your ruler and pencil. This will make them easier to measure accurately.

Reflex angles are angles that, when measured using a protractor, are **greater than 180°**.

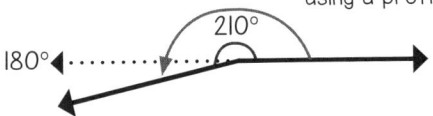

210°

180°

130

Lines

Parallel lines are always the same distance away from each other for their entire length, a little bit like the tracks that a train runs on.

Perpendicular lines meet at 90° to each other, or we might say that they intersect at 90°.

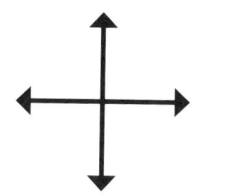

Intersecting lines cross over (or intersect) each other. The point at which lines intersect is called the point of intersection.

Common **SATs** question will show two lines intersecting and ask you to find a missing angle.

Quite often you will be given some of the other angles, so you can just subtract the known angles from 360° or 180° to find other missing angles.

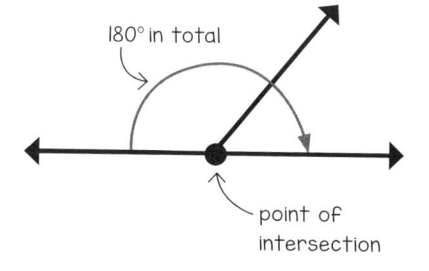

180° in total

point of intersection

SATS TIP
The key thing to remember is that if the lines cross over then you are working with 360° in a full turn. If the lines meet, you will be working with 180° in a straight line.

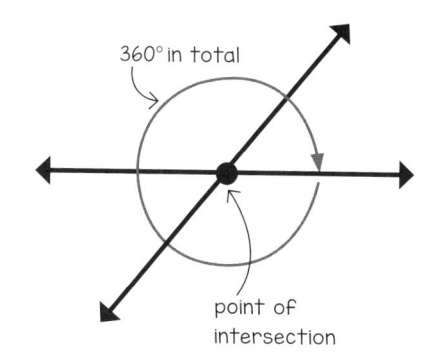

360° in total

point of intersection

REASONING

Roman numerals

Learn all of the Roman numeral facts, as these will help you answer reasoning questions that involve Roman numerals.

1	I		11	XI		200	CC
2	II		20	XX		300	CCC
3	III		30	XXX		400	CD
4	IV		40	XL		500	D
5	V		50	L		600	DC
6	VI		60	LX		700	DCC
7	VII		70	LXX		800	DCCC
8	VIII		80	LXXX		900	CM
9	IX		90	XC		1,000	M
10	X		100	C		1,001	MI

I	V	X	L	C	D	M
1	5	10	50	100	500	1,000

When smaller numbers are placed after larger numbers, for example XI (11) or VII (7), simply add them together.

When smaller numbers are placed before larger numbers, subtract the smaller number, for example CM (900) or IX (9).

NINJA TIP:
You can never have more than three of the same symbol in a row. For example III (3) or XXX (30).

Practice TASK

1) XVII = ____
2) XX = ____
3) XIV = ____
4) XXV = ____
5) LII = ____
6) XL = ____

1) 17 2) 20 3) 14 4) 25 5) 52 6) 40

132

Money

To answer reasoning questions that involve money, you need to be able to recognise the value of each coin and note.

1p 2p 5p 10p

20p 50p £1 £2

Converting pounds to pence

There are 100p in £1 so £1 is equal to 100p. Focus on converting the pounds first, then add on any pence given after the decimal place. For example, when converting £9.47, focus on the £9, which is equal to 900p, then add on the remaining 47p.

£5.00

£10.00

£20.00

£50.00

SATS TIP
SATs questions will often require you to convert between pence and pounds. For example, as part of solving a problem, you may have 334p, but the question requires that you answer in pounds. Use your knowledge of place value to work out that the answer is £3.34. 334p would be incorrect.

NINJA TIP:
Working out change can be tricky, but just remember that change is simply the difference between the money you have and the money spent. Just carry out a subtraction to work out the change.

For example, you spend £4.56 and pay with a £10 note. To calculate the change just subtract £4.56 from £10.

REASONING

133

Sequences

Sequencing questions are very common in the reasoning paper. They can be quite straightforward to answer.

NINJA TIP:
Your knowledge of your times tables can be very useful for these questions.

Continuing a sequence

The key to continuing a sequence is to work out what is happening between each of the other numbers. This will help you continue the sequence. When answering these queestions, make a note in between each number to see how the sequence is progressing and use this information to work out what comes next.

2 8 14 ☐ ☐   +6 +6

The sequence is increasing by +6 each time, so we can continue this easily.

4 7 10 ☐ ☐   +3 +3

5 10 16 ☐ ☐   +5 +6

This sequence is +5, then +6, so we can assume the next step will be +7, then +8.

Finding missing values in a sequence

With missing values, there is a little bit more trial and error. You might need to try numbers in the sequence to see whether they fit the rule. Again, make notes about what is happening between other numbers in the sequence.

☐ 17 ☐ 25 29   +4

The difference between 25 and 29 is 4. We can apply this to the sequence by subtracting 4 from 25 to see whether this fits. 25 - 4 = 21. Is the difference between 17 and 21 also 4? Yes, it is.

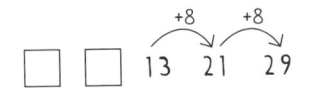

☐ ☐ 13 21 29   +8 +8

The difference between 13 and 21 is 8. The difference between 21 and 29 is also 8. To complete this sequence, subtract 8 from 13. Remember, sequences can easily end up as a negative number. In this sequence, if you continue to subtract 8, the first number in the sequence will be −3.

134

Perimeter and area

Perimeter is the distance around the outside of the shape. To calculate the perimeter, just add up all the sides of the shape.

4 cm + 4 cm + 9 cm + 9 cm = 26 cm

Area is a term used to describe the space or area found within the shape. To calculate the area of a rectangle, you just need to multiply the length by the width.

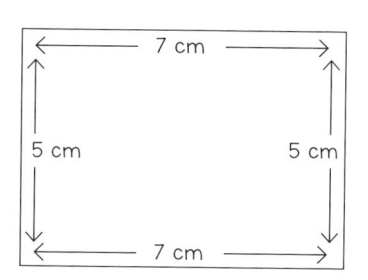

7 cm × 5 cm = 35 cm²

SATS TIP
Remember, when writing down the area, you must answer with squared (²). For example 24 cm².

Compound shapes

A compound shape is a single shape that is made up of two or more other shapes. In the example here, the larger shape is made up of two smaller rectangles.

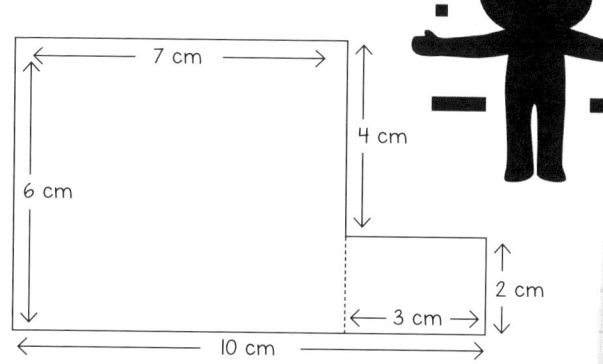

To calculate the area of a compound shape, you just need to calculate the area of the two smaller shapes and then add them together. In this example, 6 × 7 for the larger rectangle equals 42 cm², and the smaller rectangle is 3 × 2 = 6 cm². Just add these together to find the total area: 42 + 6 = 48 cm².

The perimeter of a compound shape is straightforward: just add up all the sides.

REASONING

135

Multi-step problems

Multi-step problems are usually worth two or three marks. This means you will have to carry out two or three calculations to solve the problem. Let's look at what you should be thinking about in some different multi-step problems.

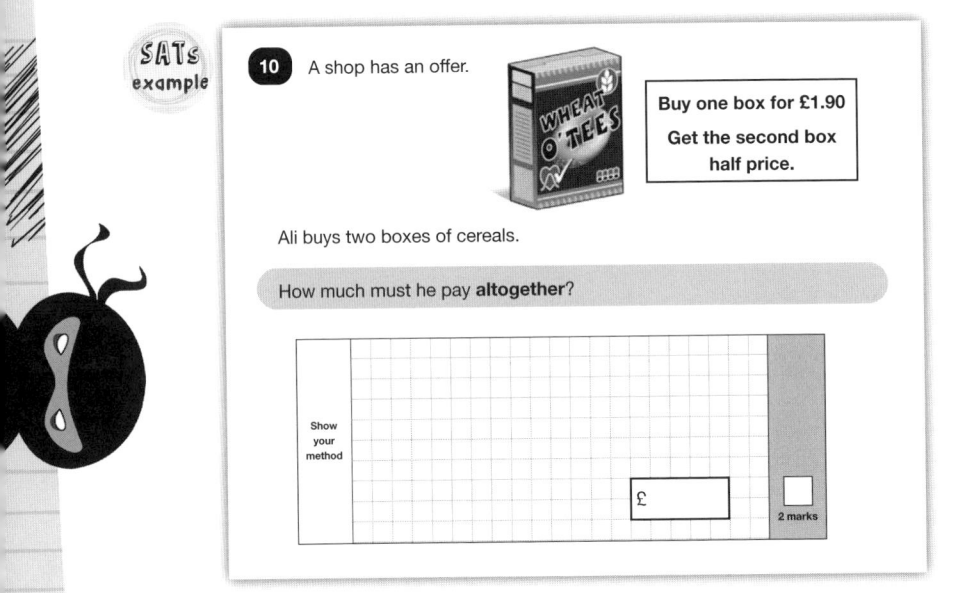

SATs example

10 A shop has an offer.

> Buy one box for £1.90
> Get the second box half price.

Ali buys two boxes of cereals.

How much must he pay **altogether**?

Show your method

£ ☐

2 marks

Notice and think: The first thing to think about is that the question is related to money. So, facts like 100p = £1 should come to mind straight away, as you may need to convert pounds to pence.

Step 1: The question says you need to buy two boxes. The first box is £1.90, but the second box is half price, so you need to halve £1.90. To make things easier, first convert pounds to pence (£1.90 = 190p). Then halve 190p. 190 ÷ 2 = 95.

Step 2: The question says, 'How much must he pay altogether?' So, you need to add together £1.90 for box one and 95p for box two. 190p + 95p = **285p**.

Notice and think: The answer box wants the answer in pounds. You must answer in the correct value to get the marks.

Step 3: Convert the pence back to pounds. 285p = £2.85. The answer is **£2.85**.

NINJA TIP:
Try to make notes as you work, so you don't have to hold all of this information in your head.

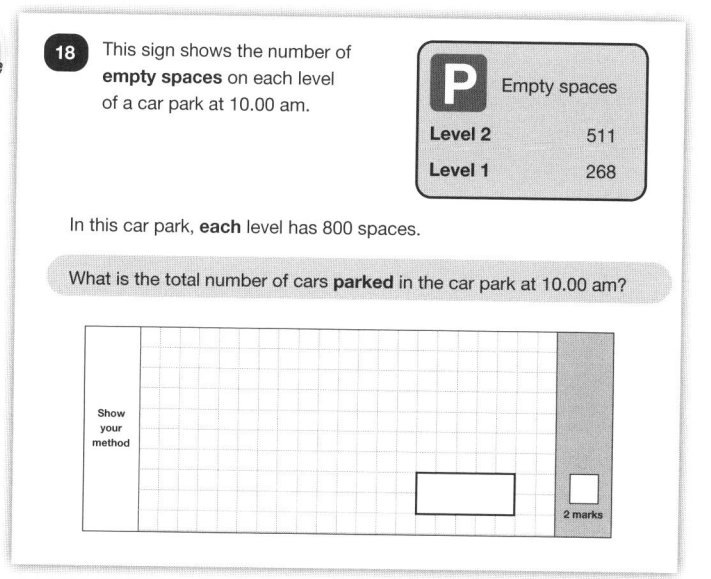

Multi-step problems

SATs example

18 This sign shows the number of **empty spaces** on each level of a car park at 10.00 am.

P Empty spaces
Level 2   511
Level 1   268

In this car park, **each** level has 800 spaces.

What is the total number of cars **parked** in the car park at 10.00 am?

Show your method

2 marks

Notice and think: Read the problem carefully. Notice that we have two three-digit numbers referencing how many empty spaces there are on each level. Each level has 800 spaces. So, the difference is how many cars are parked on each level.

Step 1: Subtract 268 from 800 (800 – 268) to calculate how many cars are parked on Level 1. There are **532** cars parked on Level 1.

Then, subtract 511 from 800 (800 – 511) to calculate how many cars are parked on Level 2. There are **289** cars parked on Level 2.

Step 2: Add **532** and **289** together to calculate the total number of cars parked at 10.00 am. The total number of parked cars is **821**.

NINJA TIP:
Remember, there are often many ways to get to an answer. In this example, you might have chosen to add 511 and 268 to find out the total number of empty spaces (779). Then you could subtract that number from 1,600 (the total number of spaces in the car park). You would get the same answer: 1,600 (spaces) – 779 (parked cars) = 821 (empty spaces).

REASONING

Multi-step problems

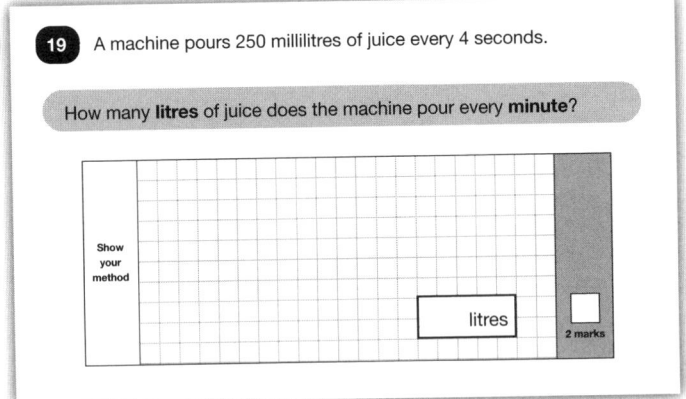

SATs example

19 A machine pours 250 millilitres of juice every 4 seconds.

How many **litres** of juice does the machine pour every **minute**?

Show your method

[ ] litres

2 marks

Notice and think: Read the problem. Notice the question is about juice, which is a liquid measured in milliletres (ml). You know 1,000 ml is equal to 1 L. The question also references time in minutes. You know that 60 seconds is equal to 1 minute.

Step 1: If the machine pours 250 ml every 4 seconds, you need to work out how many lots of 4 seconds are in one minute. 60 seconds divided by 4 seconds = 15.

Step 2: Now you know that there are 15 lots of 4 seconds in a minute and that 250ml of juice is poured every 4 seconds. So, multiply 250 ml by 15 = **3,750 ml**.

Notice and think: The answer box wants the answer in litres. You must answer in the correct value to get the marks.

Step 3: Using your knowledge of place value, you know that 1 L is equal to 1,000 ml. Convert 3,750 ml to 3.75 L by dividing by 1,000. The answer is **3.75 L**.

Multi-step problems

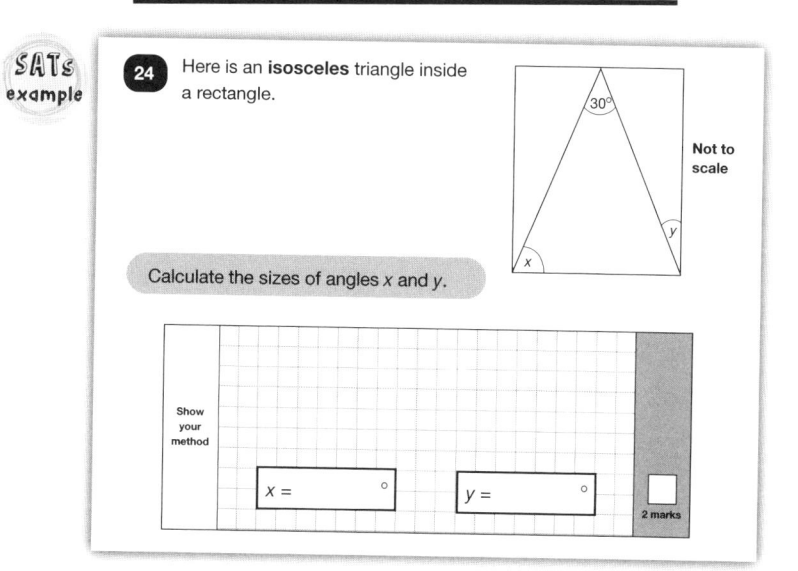

SATs example

24 Here is an **isosceles** triangle inside a rectangle.

30°

Not to scale

y

x

Calculate the sizes of angles x and y.

Show your method

$x =$ ____ ° $y =$ ____ °

2 marks

Notice and think: As soon as you see a question relating to angles, try to recall everything you can about angles, such as there are 360° in a full turn, a right angle is 90° and there are 180° in a triangle. All this information may be useful. Take notice of the shape; in this question, there is a triangle inside a rectangle (this is stated in the question). Also, the triangle is isosceles. You should know that two interior angles are equal in this type of triangle.

So, before you even start, there is a lot of information that you should be thinking about that can help you solve the problem.

Step 1: The question asks you to find x and y. x seems the logical place to start because x is inside the isosceles triangle and the total degrees inside a triangle are 180°. So, deduct 30° from 180°, and you are left with 150°. You know that x and the other interior angle are equal, so you must halve 150° to find the value of x. In this case, **$x = 75°$**.

Step 2: y is situated in the corner of a rectangle, which we know is 90°. By calculating x, you know that the angle next to y is 75°. So, y must be the difference between 90° and 75°, which is 15°. So, **$y = 15°$**.

NINJA TIP:
Always try to start with the information you have and work from there. This question relies heavily on you being able to recall a lot of information and facts that are not directly asked for.

REASONING

Use these pages to make notes about any topics you find tricky.

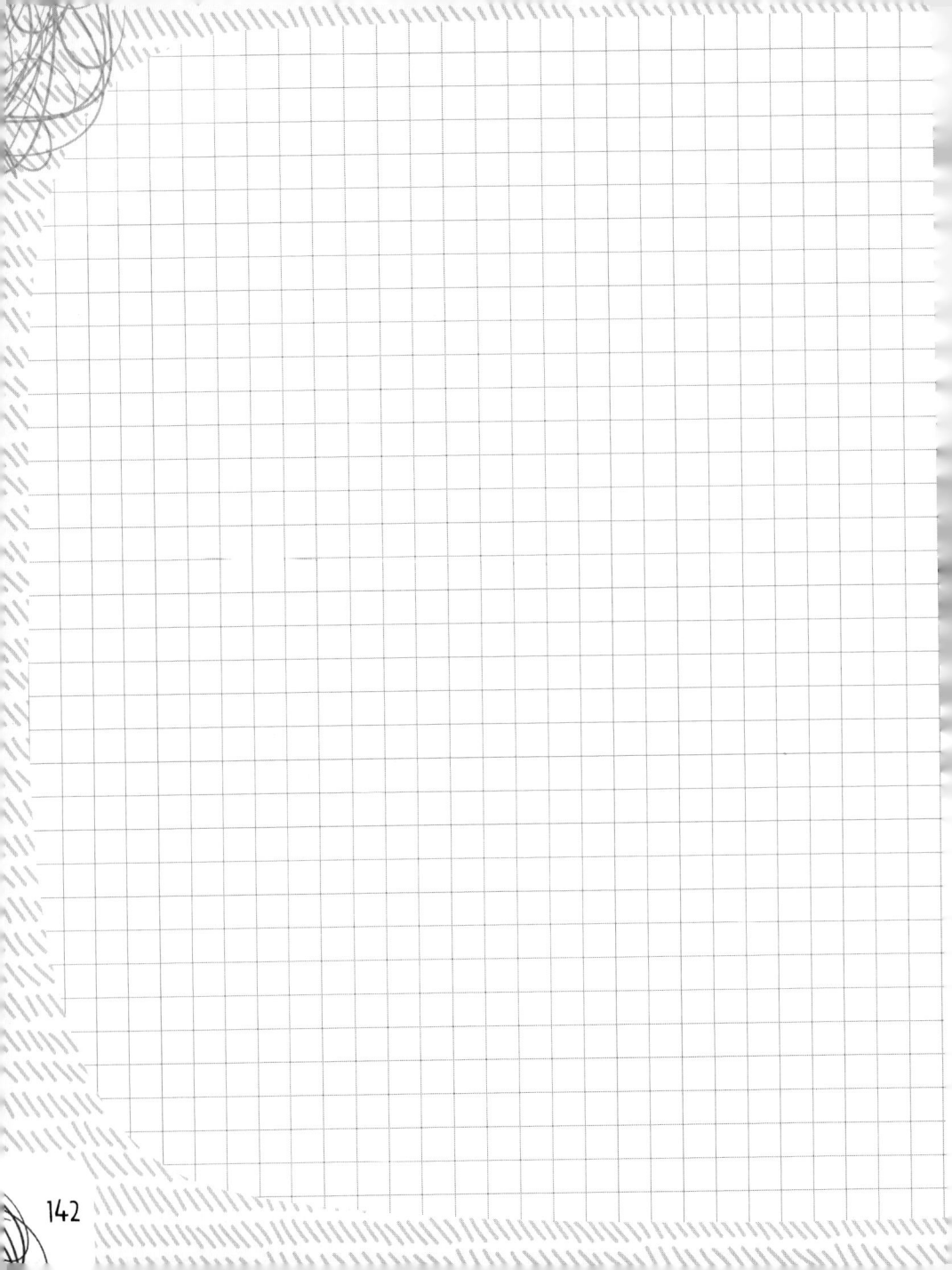

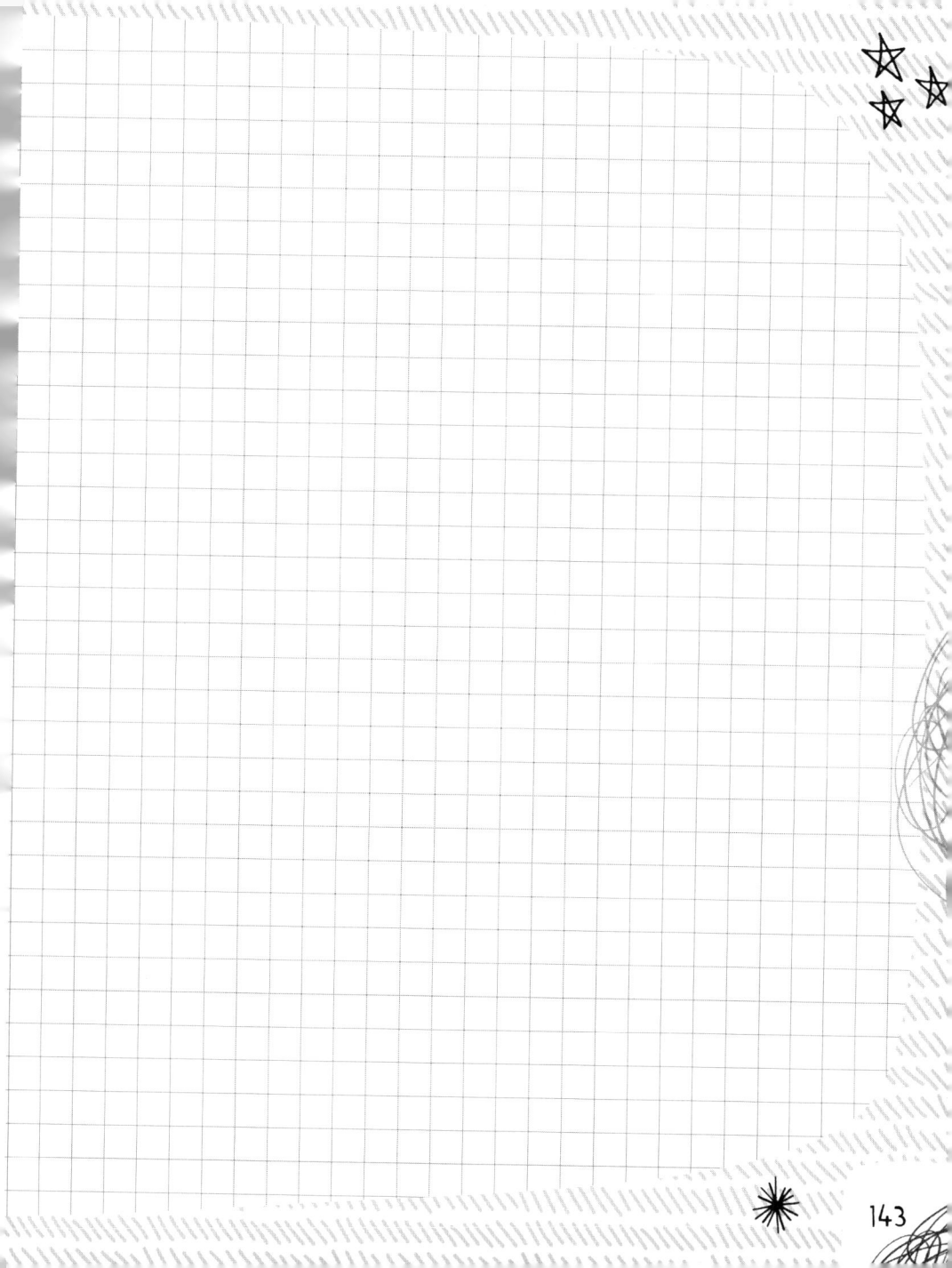